The Basic Economics

of the

Urban Racial Crisis

DANIEL R. FUSFELD
The University of Michigan

HOLT, RINEHART AND WINSTON, INC.
New York   Chicago   San Francisco   Atlanta
Dallas   Montreal   Toronto   London   Sydney

Acknowledgments

Much of this book relies very heavily on the work of other social scientists, and reference is made to them throughout. Several deserve special mention, however, because they contributed essential building blocks to the analysis presented here.

Charles Killingsworth's work on the structural elements in the labor market as a cause of unemployment, particularly his publications dealing with black employment.

The important article by R. H. Day, "Technological Change and the Share-cropper," in the *American Economic Review* for June 1967, which documented the crucial significance of technological change in southern agriculture in the late 1940s and early 1950s as an underlying cause of the urban revolt of the mid- and late 1960s.

Louis A. Ferman's research on the "irregular economy" of the urban ghetto, which circulates in mimeographed form but unfortunately has never been completed and published.

The theory of circular causation with cumulative effects developed by Gunnar Myrdal in *An American Dilemma* and spelled out in detail in Appendix 2, Volume 3 of *Asian Drama.*

The work of Barbara Bergmann on the "crowding" hypothesis concerning the economics of discrimination, building on the seminal article by Francis Y. Edgeworth in the *Economic Journal* for December 1922. This approach seems to me to be far the most useful and realistic analysis of the economic dynamics of discrimination.

The approach to urban history developed by Sam Bass Warner, Jr., which stresses the themes of multiple causation, including the economic factor, and the presence of social conflict as one outcome of the historical development of American cities.

The stimulus provided by Kenneth Boulding's work on general systems theory, which is reflected in the simple cybernetic theory of the ghetto economy developed in Chapter 4 of this book.

In addition, this whole book reflects the contributions, comments and criticisms of the students at The University of Michigan who participated in my Research Seminar on the Economics of the Urban and Racial Crisis during the years 1967–1970. So many of their ideas are to be found in these pages that this book should really be thought of as a joint product of those who participated in the seminar. Indeed, it almost seems inappropriate to have my name on a volume to which so many others have contributed so much.

As for debits, I will have to take responsibility for any errors, misstatements, or overemphasis contained in this book.

Several parts of this book have appeared elsewhere in somewhat different form. Several chapters are extensions of "The Basic Economics of the Urban and Racial Crisis," *Papers of the Philadelphia Convention*, Union for Radical Political Economics, December 1968, pp. 55-84; reprinted as URPE Reprint No. 1. That article also appeared in the *Review of Black Political Economy*, Vol. 1, No. 1 (Spring-Summer 1970) pp. 58-83, and portions of it were published in the *Proceedings of the National Black Economic Development Conference*, Detroit, Mich., April 25-27, 1967, pp. 23-25. An enlarged version of the same article appeared in *The Michigan Academician*, Vol. 11. No. 3 (Winter 1970), pp. 1-34. Much of Chapter 6 is from my paper on "Welfare Payments and the Ghetto Economy," presented at the American Association for the Advancement of Science, Boston, December 27, 1969; this paper is reprinted in Kenneth E. Boulding, Martin Pfaff and Anita B. Pfaff (eds.), *Transfers in an Urbanized Economy* (Belmont, Cal.: Wadsworth, 1972). Portions of Chapters 4 and 7 are from "The Economy of the Urban Ghetto," reprinted from John P. Crecine (ed.), *Financing the Metropolis,* Vol. 4 of the *Urban Affairs Annual Reviews* (1970), pp. 369-399, by permission of the publisher, Sage Publications, Inc.

Daniel R. Fusfeld

Ann Arbor, Michigan
January 1973

CONTENTS

The Basic Issues

The impetus for writing this book was a conviction that the conventional theory about the nature and causes of the urban racial problem in the United States is largely wrong; that the remedies based on an incorrect diagnosis are largely irrelvant; and that unless we get at basic causes the problems will remain unresolved. My chief quarrel with the usual approach is its failure to recognize that the chief causes of the racial problem are economic, that those causes lie deep in the heart of the economic institutions of this country, and that they will not be eliminated without fundamental changes in economic relationships. In that sense, this book is an indictment of the economic system as a whole, seen from the perspective of one of the problems that gnaws at its vitals.

The key point was expressed in down-to-earth language by an anonymous union official:

> Sure, the Kerner Commission Report they read to us from was right; sure there's been racism in this country since it was founded. But the slaves weren't brought over here because white racists wanted them nearby to shout at, and the colored weren't kept on those plantations for that reason, and they're not sweeping floors and working in kitchens or any other place for that reason. They were *labor*, labor when they were brought over here, and they are labor now—a pool of cheap labor, and that's what the big boys who own plantations or corporations (or a big house they need kept clean) have always wanted: plenty of people desperate enough to do mean, tough, unpleasant work for cheap wages, or no wages at all.[1]

Exploitation of low-wage labor is the chief economic basis of the urban ghetto. Yet the ghetto is more than that. It is an economic subsystem which preserves the inferior position of the minorities in our midst. The ghetto reproduces from one generation to the next the economic relationships that preserve an exploitive social order. Yet the ghetto itself and its ties to the rest of the economy change and adapt as conflict erupts and the larger economic system responds. This book is an effort to disentangle the complex web of

---

[1]Robert Coles, "Understanding White Racists," *New York Review of Books,* Vol. XVII, No. 11 (Dec. 30, 1971), p. 15.

economic forces that create our urban ghettos, that preserve them while changing them, that keep our racial minorities in bondage while adapting just enough to maintain the essential elements of an exploitive economic order.

The prevailing philosophy sees the issue differently. The traditional liberal view is that white racial attitudes have closed opportunities for blacks and other minority groups, while minorities have been denied the education to develop the skills necessary for advancement. The remedies are obvious: change white attitudes, if necessary by enforcing nondiscriminatory practices in employment and housing, and provide minority groups with education and training to develop their latent abilities. Meanwhile, ameliorative measures, such as welfare and health programs, improved housing, and other subsidies, can improve matters and reduce unrest, until both whites and blacks have been changed enough to defuse racial tensions. Underneath this approach is the assumption that the problem lies with people rather than with basic economic institutions.

Militant minority groups, on the other hand, recognize the exploitive nature of the economic system in which they are the victims and, for the most part, identify the source of the problem as the prevailing system of economic and political power. Their resistance to ameliorative measures and their efforts to use such measures for purposes of .agitiation stem from a sometimes intuitive and sometimes conscious perception of the fact that amelioration serves to preserve their exploitation and that of their children.

Meanwhile, in the background is the "law and order" movement. It is willing to use the liberal reforms to ease tensions, but its chief instrument is repression of the violence, crime, and disorder that persists in erupting from a society torn by conflict. Concerned primarily with preserving positions of economic advantage, it is quite willing to have a select few rise from the oppressed minorities into professional, managerial, and white-collar employment and through "black capitalism" into business ownership as long as the economic reality of a low-wage work force is maintained. The political representatives of this point of view already are moving to take over and modify the programs of the conventional approach, such as welfare reform, to achieve conservative goals. The undoubtedly sincere humanitarianism of the conventional liberal finds itself the bedfellow of social forces bent on strengthening an inhuman system.

The place of blacks in the American economic system has always been that of a captive nation from which a few have been able to escape. Slavery was followed by a system of sharecropping and debt tenure in the rural South, which was succeeded by an era of crowding into low-wage menial occupations in the urban North. Each system of coerced labor was less severe than the earlier one, and the constraints which enforced them were successively more informal. In that sense, each step represented an improvement. But improvement took place only during periods of national trauma: the Civil War, the upheavals of the two World Wars, and the depression of the 1930s. Will it take another national time of troubles to break the bonds of the present ghetto economy? Or will we be able to eliminate the inequities and exploitation that keep our minorities in their economic Bastille?

The economic life of the inner city is, in one sense, a world apart, differing and separated from the affluent world that surrounds it. In another sense, it is inextricably intertwined with that surrounding world. If our captive nations are to be finally freed, both the ghetto economy and the surrounding affluent world will have to be changed. That need not happen, and the problems and conflicts can remain indefinitely. On the other hand, we can recognize the seriousness and depth of the problem and seek out the changes in the distribution of income and wealth, and in the structure of power, that are needed. For one point should be clear from the pages that follow: amelioration will not do—it merely serves to perpetuate an exploitive set of economic relationships. It is a temporary strategy at best, that can only hold the line until more fundamental changes are made.

CHAPTER 1

The Ghetto and the City

American cities present a series of paradoxes. Urban areas are growing larger and contain an increasing portion of the population; yet at the same time their density is diminishing, and urban sprawl is growing. On the one hand, cities are the dynamic center of the economy and support a thriving cultural activity; on the other, the central cores are disintegrating and deteriorating. Cities are integrated economic units in which the various parts are highly articulated and closely integrated with each other; but in other respects cities are full of conflict, animosity, and hatred. These paradoxes are the outward aspect of the malaise that grips American urban life. They are manifestations of the urban crisis of our time.

American urban areas have serious problems that remain unresolved, not because the means for their solution are unavailable, but because the social and economic conflicts that are built into American society prevent us from taking effective action. At the heart of that conflict are extremes of wealth and poverty exacerbated by the fact that racial differences and economic differences overlap each other. The inner portions of the central cities are poor *and* black or Latin, with other minority groups represented also, while the suburbs are affluent *and* largely white. The result is continuing warfare between central city and suburb, rich and poor, white and black; a warfare that is sometimes muted but often overt. The urban crisis is an urban racial crisis with deep roots in economic relationships as well as racial attitudes.

The Ghetto

In the heart of the central cities are the ghettos. They are peopled largely by blacks, Puerto Ricans, Spanish-speaking Americans, and other minority groups—and by some whites, mostly older people. It is here that poverty reigns. It is here that despair brings drug addiction and crime and where anger leads to militancy and violence.

The ghetto has three chief characteristics. Its people are clearly recognizable as racial or national minorities. It is poor. And there are cultural differences, which are far less obvious and much more difficult to define. For example, black cultural patterns and values—

which include such intangibles as one's view of the world as well as attitudes and family structure—differ from those of the dominant white Protestant and white Catholics groups or the white Jewish minority. They also differ from the Latin Catholic racially mixed culture of Spanish-speaking Americans. Whatever may be one's view of cultural values, we must recognize that conflicts between cultural patterns are as much a part of the urban racial crisis as conflicts between races and conflicts between the affluent and the poor.

Although urban ghettos can be defined in conceptual terms, it is extremely difficult to define them in terms of geographical boundaries useful for purposes of analysis. Careful observation enables one to draw boundary lines, but they seldom coincide with census tracts or areas, or any of the other units for which data are available. Furthermore, the continuing spread of ghetto areas and efforts at urban renewal change the geographical base and add to the problem of definition and analysis.[1]

Nevertheless, it is possible to estimate the scope of the problem. Anthony Downs has made an estimate of the number of persons in our urban ghettos, first, on the basis of race and, second, on the basis of income, as of the mid-1960s. In 1966 there were about 12.5 million nonwhites living in all U.S. central cities, of whom 12.1 million were black. Of these ghetto residents, almost 40 percent were members of family units with incomes below the poverty level, which in 1964 was $3,300 annually for a family of four.[2]

Based on income, the size of our urban ghettos is somewhat smaller. A little over 10 million persons with incomes below the poverty level lived in the central cities in 1964. Of these, about 56 percent were white and 44 percent nonwhite.[3] We do not know what proportion of the whites were Spanish-speaking, but a large portion of the population of urban ghettos are persons with "Spanish surnames," to use the current official terminology.

Whether defined by race or by poverty income, then, the urban

[1]Geographical analyses of the black ghetto and slum areas are found in R. L. Morrill, "The Negro Ghetto: Problems and Alternatives," *Geographical Review*, Vol. 55, No. 3 (July 1965), pp. 339-361; J. R. Seeley, "The Slum: Its Nature, Use and Users," *Journal of the American Institute of Planners*, Vol. 25, No. 1 (February 1959), pp. 7-14; C. L. Stokes, "A Theory of Slums," *Land Economics*, Vol. 38, No. 3 (August 1962), pp. 187-197.

[2]Anthony Downs, "Alternative Futures for the American Ghetto," *Daedalus*, Vol. 97, No. 4 (Fall 1968), pp. 1331-78; reprinted in Downs, *Urban Problems and Prospects* (Chicago: Markham Publishing, 1970), pp. 27-74.

[3]Quoted by Downs, *ibid.*, from the Report of *The National Advisory Commission on Civil Disorders* (Washington: U. S. Government Printing Office, 1964), p. 127.

ghetto population comprises perhaps 5 to 7 percent of the nation. It includes 8 to 10 percent of the population of our metropolitan areas. These are minimal estimates, however. When the near-poor are included, and we define the urban ghettos as those census tracts in which family incomes average less than $7,500 annually, they include 20 to 25 percent of the population of U.S. metropolitan areas. The great bulk of this population is made up of racial minorities— mostly black and Latin—and much of the white population is either aged or very young. The fact that it is largely a minority population makes its position weak when majorities decide. The fact that it is a rejected minority, generally looked down upon by the more affluent majority makes its position even weaker. Racial and cultural differences make identification of the ghetto easier but add to the difficuties in finding solutions.

Long-term Trends and the Current Crisis

Today's urban and racial crisis has its roots in three long-range problems: the changing nature of American cities, the persistence of poverty, and the failure of the American social system to make an equal place for black people. These three problems have been with us for a long time, and they will remain indefinitely into the future. Together they would have brought an urban and racial problem of major proportions even if other events had not accelerated the situation into a crisis.

The Changing City

Modern technology has brought some fundamental changes to American cities. Decentralization of both manufacturing and population has been a long-term trend, clearly evident for the last fifty years. Prior to World I cities developed around railroad and port facilities. The development of mass rail transit, which brought both people and goods into the industrial core, gave further impetus to the growth of the cities. But after World War I, motor transportation set into motion a countermovement. It made decentralization possible for both manufacturing and wholesale distribution. In addition, mass production industries using one-story plants for continuous-flow processes required large tracts, which were difficult and expensive to assemble in downtown areas. The availability of cheap land and cheap transportation enabled goods production to move from the central city core into the suburbs.[4] The automobile enabled people to move too.

Urban decentralization was slowed by the depression of the 1930s and the outbreak of World War II. For a time the war tended to lock urban growth into traditional central locations. After World War II, however, decentralization trends reasserted themselves more strongly than ever. A backlog of technological change that had piled up for fifteen years from 1930 through 1945 began to be rapidly applied, and industry expanded at unprecedented rates. People, much manufacturing and wholesaling, and a great deal of retail trade were suburbanized far from the central cities.

As industry moved to less crowded areas, central cities increasingly became the center for administration, finance, recreation, and certain other types of services. Except for the most efficient or the most backward of the old plants, generally only the low-wage industries, such as clothing manufacture, remained, drawn by the surplus labor of overcrowded slums. For the most part, high-wage industrial jobs deserted the cities.

The changes in the city brought important changes in employment opportunities for the low-income residents of the central city areas. Women have found jobs to be relatively easily available in the administrative and service industries of the downtown area, in places served by public transportation facilities. Men seeking industrial jobs for the most part, however, must rely on automobiles or inadequate public transportation to the outlying industrial areas.

A substantial portion of the decentralization of cities was subsidized by the federal government. Movement of people was assisted by subsidies to housing, particularly by mortgage guarantees under the GI Bill and by the FHA, (Federal Housing Administration) while the Federal National Mortgage Association assured the housing industry of an adequate flow of capital for whatever construction the

---

[4]Some mass production—continuous—flow industries had always been located in suburban industrial centers. The steel industry in the Pittsburgh area is a good example of pre-World War I industrial development which followed the decentralization pattern. Steel brought its work force out to the industrial suburbs, into the steel towns, as well. Some other large product assembly industries followed the same pattern, the Pullman Company for example, and Pullman, Illinois.

industry undertook. Federal highway programs also promoted suburbanization of both people and industry. After World War II the automobile became an essential item for those not living in the central cities, regardless of their incomes. As a result, urban and suburban mass transit systems were allowed to deteriorate: much of the public now no longer needed or wanted them.

Decentralization also had the effect of reducing the financial resources of central cities. One of the initial advantages of moving to the suburbs was low taxes on property as well as relatively low costs of land. Low tax rates, in turn, mean relatively meager urban services—volunteer rather than paid professional fire departments, for example, or weak public library systems. As people and industry located in the suburbs, there was a smaller tax base to provide for the expanding normal needs of the central cities. Furthermore, as we shall shortly see, the migration and growth of the black population was putting additional strains on city budgets in some entirely new ways.

These economic trends were exacerbated by an archaic political structure. City boundaries were not extended to include the growing suburbs, and a multiplicity of political jurisdictions made metropolitan problem solving extremely difficult. Inadequate aid to the cities came from state governments, for domination of state legislatures by rural interests was the general rule. Even the redistricting of legislatures in the 1960s has not helped cities significantly: the balance of power has been placed in the suburbs, and people there originally fled the cities and look upon them with suspicion and fear. Even at the national level the influence of the suburbs and rural areas has been dominant. Most federal programs until very recently have ignored the cities and provided aid to the suburbs instead.

The Persistence of Poverty

American cities have always had contrasts of wealth and poverty. Slums, present from the very beginning, have served two functions. They have been temporary stopping places for immigrants from abroad and from rural areas who were starting the journey upward in American society. But they have also been the end of the line for failures, for those who were society's dropouts and rejects.

American slums, or "urban poverty areas," have consistently had bad housing, crowded living conditions, poor education, bad health conditions, high death rates, inadequate public facilities, high crime rates, and police brutality. Present conditions are nothing new, although they may be both more widespread and concentrated more heavily for a single racial group.

The economy of urban poverty areas has always featured high rates of unemployment, low wage rates, and an "irregular" economy partially inside and partially outside the law. Manpower is the major economic resource of the slums, and this manpower has always been relatively unskilled and uneducated when compared with the manpower resources of the economy as a whole. Permanent depression and the syndrome of economic underdevelopement have been characteristic of slum areas through the years.

The conditions of life in a poor community tend to reinforce and preserve poverty. Low incomes are the result of low productivity, which is promoted, in turn, by poor diet and poor health, two of the chief hallmarks of poverty. Low incomes mean crowded and unsanitary housing, which leads to bad health and low productivity. Poverty breeds crime, and a police record makes it difficult for a man to get a decent job, which reinforces the poverty that led to the criminal behavior in the first place. Poverty leads to difficulties with the credit system, which, in turn, leads to difficulties in holding jobs (many employers fire workers for repeated wage garnishments by creditors). A poor neighborhood often has little political strength, which leads to inadequate public facilities—poor schools, libraries, hospitals, and other public services. Lack of public services reinforces the poor health and education which are basic causes of low productivity. The circular causation of poverty—"the poor are poor because they are poor"—is one of the reasons for its persistence.

The urban poverty areas of earlier times differed in two important ways from today's. First, the European nationality groups were not segregated. Although nationality groups tended to cluster together, the clusters were usually not large. The more common pattern was for nationality groups to be intermingled with each other in the same city block and even within the same tenement house. Second, most ethnic groups other than the Negro have in part bypassed the slums. For example, although most Irish immigrants moved first into urban slum areas, others did not. Some moved directly into higher income and more respectable parts of the cities. As a result, when the slum Irish moved up economically and out of the slums physically, they found themselves moving into urban areas where others like themselves had already broken the ground. The older residents knew what Irishmen were like because they already had some as neighbors. Other groups followed similar patterns and some, like the Germans, largely bypassed the big city slums.

Neither of these two patterns applied to the Negro. The black parts of slum areas tended to be segregated from the white from the earliest days, and as the black population of cities rose, the black sector of the slums became more crowded and expanded into nearby white-occupied areas. As the blacks moved in, the whites moved out. New York's Harlem of the 1920s and 1930s is perhaps the classic example of this development. Furthermore, black people seldom bypassed the black areas of cities even when their economic status might have permitted it. By the 1960s the black ghetto comprised both slum and nonslum areas. As a result, today's problems of urban poverty and racial ghettos, although not synonymous, are inextricably intertwined.

White Racism

Other racial and national groups have escaped the vicious circle of slum life by pulling themselves out into the progressive, higher income sectors of the economy. Black people have largely been unable to do so because of the racial attitudes of white people. Blacks have always been at the bottom of the economic ladder. Low-wage, unskilled jobs with little or no opportunity for advancement, limited and inadequate educational opportunities, and restricted entry into skilled trades closed off economic opportunities in the blue-collar occupations. Administrative positions and white-collar jobs were unavailable because of the generally WASPish nature of business leadership and its attitudes (which discriminated against Catholics, Jews, and recent immigrants as well, although to a lesser extent). Jobs for blacks in the federal government were limited to those at the bottom level, first by the alliance of conservative southern congressmen with conservative northern Republicans (which was first hammered out in 1876), and later in Democratic administrations by the strength of the southern wing of the party. For example, the Supreme Court decisions which validated the "separate but equal" doctrine came from courts dominated by conservative Republican justices after the so-called Compromise of 1876, which gave the presidency to Hayes in exchange for the return of state government control in the South to white conservatives. Most of the official segregation in the city of Washington, D. C., and the federal government was introduced in the Democratic administration of Woodrow Wilson.

The history of white racism in the United States is yet to be written, but the general outlines can be sketched.[5] Racist attitudes seem to have grown in intensity and breadth from the 1880s into the 1920s. This development coincided with overseas imperialism in both the United States and Europe. In the United States it led to passage of Jim Crow laws, lynchings in the South, violence against blacks in the North, and discrimination against blacks in employment and labor unions. Some historians place the peak of this development in the mid-1920s. It was supported by the appearance of an ideology and pseudoscience which held that the white European races were superior to others. Philosophers like Nietzsche, scholars like William Z. Ripley and the early physical anthropologists, while not overtly racist like Gobineau, H. S. Chamberlain, and Homer Lea, helped create the intellectual environment which enabled racial discrimination to go largely unquestioned even by the intellectual community.

A reaction to racism did begin in the years before World War I, marked perhaps by the founding of the NAACP (National Association for the Advancement of Colored People) in 1909 and the National Urban League in 1911. It has proceeded unevenly ever since, picking up speed after World War II with the civil rights movement, the pathbreaking Supreme Court decisions, and congressional civil rights legislation. With all of its false starts, steps backward, and explosive social tensions, the United States has taken a path away from the racism of the years before World War I. At the very least, the old

---

[5]Several books have partially closed the gap in American historical scholarship on racial attitudes, including C. Vann Woodward, *The Strange Career of Jim Crow* (New York: Oxford University Press, 1955); David B. Davis, *The Problem of Slavery in Western Culture* (Ithaca, N. Y.: Cornell University Press, 1965); Winthrop D. Jordan, *White Over Black: American Attitudes Toward the Negro, 1550-1812* (Chapel Hill: University of North Carolina Press, 1968); George M. Fredrickson, *The Inner Civil War: Northern Intellectnals and the Crisis of the Union* (New York: Harper & Row, 1965), and *The Black Image in the White Mind: The Debate on Afro-American Character and Destiny, 1817-1914* (New York: Harper & Row, 1971); and Constance M. Green, *The Secret City: A History of Race Relations in the Nation's Capital* (Princeton, N. J.: Princeton University Press, 1967).

attitudes and practices are no longer respectable. Nevertheless, the entrenched economic patterns of the past have persisted, particularly discrimination in employment,[6] housing, and labor unions.[7] The attack on these economic aspects of racial discrimination has been late in coming and has not yet had significant results. Perhaps a beginning has been made.

Sources of Urban Conflict

Racial animosities are the most obvious and troubling sources of conflict in American cities at the present time. But there are other sources of the antagonisms that divide urban America.

One is the wide economic disparaties that divide metropolitan areas into three different communities of the poor and near-poor, the affluent middle-income majority, and the rich. Cities are divided geographically by income levels, with the three income groups living separately, working separately, and spending their leisure time separately. An informal economic apartheid has developed in American urban areas.

The central city ghettos and the surrounding areas, which contain between 20 and 25 percent of the city's population, are where the poor and near-poor live. These parts of the urban area are close to industrial districts and the older downtown commercial areas, although most metropolitan areas also have a few scattered islands of poverty and near-poverty in the suburbs. Average annual family incomes in the central city ghettos are below $7,500.

One very significant aspect of urban development in recent years has been the spread of ghettoization into the suburbs. In some instances a nucleus was provided by the remnants of a black ghetto that had formed around suburban World War II industrial plants. But the chief reason for growth of suburban ghettos has been the

[6]The results of racism on the place of blacks in the economy is summarized in Arthur M. Ross, "The Negro in the American Economy," in A. M. Ross and Herbert Hill (eds.), *Employment, Race and Poverty* (New York: Harcourt Brace Jovanovich, 1967), pp. 3-47. See also Dale E. Hiestand, *Economic Growth and Employment Opportunities for Minorities* (New York: Columbia University Press, 1964).

[7]See Sterling D. Spero and Abram L. Harris, *The Black Worker* (New York: Columbia University Press, 1931), and Ray Marshall, *The Negro and Organized Labor* (New York: John Wiley, 1965).

process of urban decentralization itself. As economic activity moved into the suburbs, the low-wage, menial labor force moved with it. These workers found places to settle nearby, and ghettoization began. The suburban ghettos are living demonstrations of the proposition that ghettos are one outcome of the present economic organization, have deep roots in the pattern of income distribution, and appear wherever American urban society spreads.

The middle-income majority live in the suburbs and in the central city areas surrounding the central core of poverty. Average family incomes in those parts of the metropolitan area range between $7,500 and $15,000 annually. The families earning these incomes encompass some 70 to 75 percent of the urban population. These are the Americans whose well-scrubbed life is celebrated on TV as the American Way. They live in single-family homes or in neat garden apartment developments, filled with electrical appliances and surrounded by lawns on tree-shaded streets, with late-model cars in the driveway. Their children go to college and thereby gain a ticket of admittance to the race for economic success, in which few fail to achieve the moderate incomes that enable them to at least replicate their parents' middle-income way of life.

The wealthy are relative few in number. Only some 5 to 10 percent of urban families live in areas in which family incomes average over $15,000 annually. Those parts of the metropolitan area are either the blue-stocking downtown areas of the city with luxury apartment houses or the country-club suburbs with large homes. Here live those who manage the American economy and make the decisions, who have the revenues from accumulated wealth, and who dominate the economy's financial stucture.

These economic disparaties create separate ways of life. American economic classes live apart, have different forms of recreation in different places, and seldom come into contact with each other on the job. The corporation executive does not eat lunch with a bookkeeper, nor does he invite the janitor to his home for dinner. The plant manager does not sit down with an assembly-line worker at his coffee break or go bowling with a sweeper. Separation based on economic disparaties is the rule.

Economic differences are supplemented by cultural differences. The old view of American cities as melting pots in which people of greatly different national and cultural backgrounds were transformed into Americans similar to each other is now seen to be inadequate. Instead, cities are seen as places in which successive waves of immigrants strengthened their own national and cultural values while they were also becoming Americans. The result was the appearance of a society of multicultural diversity. Several different patterns of attitudes and value systems emerged, which social psychologists now can identify as white Protestant, white Catholic, and white Jewish.[8]

The white Protestant culture was brought with the first English settlers. The other two developed during the great era of immigration from 1840 to 1910. The immigrants came into the urban slums of those days, where, surrounded by a hostile world and living in unfamiliar surroundings, they reacted by sticking together and trying to preserve their common heritage. They formed their own religious and fraternal organizations, emphasized family solidarity, founded newspapers in their native languages, and developed a political awareness that led to bloc voting. Crowded into low-wage occupations and discriminated against by white Protestant America, they came together and reasserted their identity. Many of these earlier immigrant groups retained that solidarity even after they escaped the ghettos by developing their own communities or neighborhoods within the larger city, maintaining separate parochial school systems in whole or in part and establishing organizations that preserved their cultural patterns. By the third quarter of the twentieth century these cultural patterns began to intermingle geographically in the rapidly spreading suburbs, but they, nevertheless, retained their identity.

Blacks and Latins are now following the same path, and for essentially the same reasons. Crowded into slums and segregated from the main stream of American life, they are developing a fuller

---

[8]The evidence for multicultural diversity is to be found in work by social psychologists, including Ruby Jo Reeves Kennedy, "Single or Triple Melting Pot?" *American Journal of Sociology*, Vol. XLIX (Jan. 1944) pp. 331-339; Will Herberg, *Protestant, Catholic, Jew: An Essay in American Religious Sociology* (Garden City, N. Y.: Doubleday, 1955); Gerhard E. Lenski, *The Religious Factor: A Sociological Study of Religion's Impact on Politics, Economics and Family Life* (Garden City, N. Y.: Doubleday, 1961); Edward O. Laumann, "The Social Structure of Religious and Ethnoreligious Groups in a Metropolitan Community: A Smallest Space Analysis," *American Sociological Review*, Vol. XXXIV (April 1969). The leading historian of U.S. immigrants adopted the schema of four socioreligious categories in American society: Oscar Handlin, "Historical Perspectives on the American Ethnic Group," *Daedalus*, Vol. XC (Spring 1961), pp. 220-232. Continued development of multicultural diversity was predicted in Nathan Glazer and Daniel Moynihan, *Beyond the Melting Pot: The Negroes, Puerto Ricans, Jews, Italians and Irish of New York City* (Cambridge: M.I.T. Press, 1963), which has been the most influential book in breaking down the old melting-pot thesis.

awareness of their own cultures and are developing political strength. A fivefold pattern of diverse cultures is emerging in urban America, with a black Protestant and a Latin Catholic culture supplementing the three earlier ones. But there is one difference. The earlier cultural differences were all variations among racially homogeneous whites. The two emerging cultural patterns are racially differentiated from the other three. Blacks have always been subjected to racial segregation in this country, and one characteristic feature of the Latin Catholic culture is its background of liberal attitudes toward racial mixtures. The black and Latin cultures bring the new element of racial differences to the multicultural pattern of present-day urban metropolitan regions.

A strong foundation for social and economic conflict has been built in urban America. Economic disparities strengthened by an informal economic apartheid are supplemented by substantial cultural differences based on religion and nationality. To these must be added racial differences and antagonisms. Under the surface of the apparently smooth functioning of the daily life of the city lies a potentially explosive conflict. Sometimes it emerges as individual acts of violence, sometimes as riots. But it is always there in the less obvious form of suspicion, hostility, and hatred.

CHAPTER 2

The Black Migration and Population Explosion

Changing cities, poverty, and racism developed into serious problems for the United States in the post-World War II years, particularly since their impact converged in the low-income slums of central cities. In the early 1950s the problems were vastly intensified by the large-scale, unanticipated, and even now largely unappreciated, migration of black people from the rural South to northern cities. And these problems remained unsolved in the 1970s.

Agricultural Technology and the Black Migration

The roots of today's crisis are to be found in a sudden transformation of southern agriculture which culminated in the 1950s. For a number of years prior to 1950 a changing technology was eliminating hand labor from southern agriculture. The old sharecropping system was on the way out as tractors and cultivators replaced men. By 1949 most hand labor had been eliminated from everything but summer weeding and fall harvesting. This development was the first stage of the process which pushed the bulk of black farm workers out of southern agriculture. Needed only for temporary or seasonal labor, many black sharecroppers lost their homesteads and moved into southern towns and cities, although some did go north, continuing the migration which had been going on for decades. In the southern towns the black worker was poor, but, available for seasonal and harvest labor, he subsisted and stayed in the South.

Then disaster struck. Machine harvesting of cotton and corn was introduced on a large scale in 1950, and there was a substantial expansion of soybean acreage (which uses little labor). The result was a huge decline in the use of labor. For example, in the space of only three years from 1949 to 1952 the use of unskilled agricultural labor in twenty Mississippi delta counties fell by 72 percent, and five years later it was down to only 10 percent of the 1949 level.[1]

---

[1]The best account of this two-stage push of black workers out of southern agriculture is R. H. Day, "Technological Change and the Sharecropper," *American Economic Review*, Vol. LVII; No. 3 (June, 1967), pp. 427-449. The problem continued with somewhat reduced intensity into the 1960s. See the following articles by Michael J. Piore, "Negro Workers in the Mississippi Delta; Problems of Displacement and Adjustment," *Proceedings of the Industrial Relations Research Association*, (Winter 1967), pp.

The black migration of the 1950s occurred simultaneously with other technological changes that made the economic position of the black migrants particularly difficult. The rest of American agriculture also experienced large increases in productivity that pushed many farmers and potential farmers off the land and into urban areas. Mechanization of coal mining caused a large white migration out of Appalachia. These groups had an advantage over blacks, because they were largely white and had easier access to jobs. Not that jobs were easy to get. As we will shortly see, other economic changes in the 1950s closed off many economic opportunities to new entrants into the urban labor market, with a particularly severe impact on blacks.

The Earlier Black Migration

The migration of blacks to the North began on a substantial scale in the second decade of the twentieth century. In the early decades of the movement it was stimulated by both the push of deprivation and the pull of opportunity. The decline of cotton agriculture in the South exerted an outward push. Restrictive immigration laws after 1910 closed off an important source of low-wage unskilled labor for northern industry. Continued economic growth tended to pull low-wage white workers into higher level jobs, and blacks responded to the pull of the economic opportunities they vacated at the bottom of the labor market in the north. The migration that began under the impact of these long-range forces was greatly accelerated during World War I, with jobs in war industries the chief attraction. Blacks continued to move north during the relatively prosperous 1920s, but the great depression of the 1930s greatly slowed down the migration. In all, there was a net migration from the South of some 1,800,000 blacks in the three decades of 1910 to 1940.[2] Arriving in the northern cities, the migrants were crowded into low-wage occupations and the black ghettos of our major cities expanded to accommodate them.[3]

World War II greatly speeded up the black migration. Jobs were

366-374; "Changes in the Mississippi Agricultural Economy and the Problems of Displaced Negro Farmworkers," *American Journal of Psychotherapy*, Vol. XXII, No. 4 (October 1968), pp. 592-601; "Memorandum on the Economic Problems of Negroes in the Delta of Mississippi," NAACP Legal Defense and Education Fund (mimeo, n.d.).

[2]C. Horace Hamilton, "The Negro Leaves the South," *Demography*, Vol. 1, No. 1 (1964), pp. 273-295, brings together a great deal of data on the black migration.

[3]The northern ghettos are described in Robert C. Weaver, *The Negro Ghetto* (New York: Harcourt, Brace 1948); St. Clair Drake and Horace R. Cayton, *Black Metropolis: A*

available in the mass production war industries operating under cost-plus contracts. Training programs fitted new workers to jobs in which the skills had been simplified and broken into their component parts, and federal antidiscrimination measures opened up new opportunities. After the war expanded production of durable consumer goods, such as automobiles, kept the migration going. The Korean war continued the demand into the early 1950s, but on a much reduced scale. The black migration of the 1940s, drawn by economic opportunity, was far greater than anything that had gone before. Fully 1,600,000 blacks moved from the South to the North in the decade—almost as many as in the previous thirty years.

The immediate postwar years saw the development of some serious urban ghetto problems of a new sort, however. With the closing of wartime industries in which many blacks had found employment, some areas began to feel the impact of large-Scale mass unemployment that persisted almost indefinitely. The so-called "Paradise Valley" area of Detroit became a seriously depressed area and was the city's first candidate for a major urban renewal program when the automobile and machinery industries reconverted to civilian production in the late 1940s. Also in Michigan, the suburban ghettos of Inkster and Willow Village, which had developed around the Willow Run bomber plant, retrogressed into slum conditions. Perhaps the most spectacular examples of urban poverty areas created by the ending of military production were in the San Francisco area: Hunter's Point (based on Bethlehem Steel Company's shipyard nearby) and North Richmond (based on the Kaiser shipyard at Richmond). Both of these communities were geographically and politically separate from the surrounding areas. Unemployment caused by closing the war plants was heavily concentrated, the unemployed did not disperse into the surrounding communities, and slums of the worst sort quickly developed.

Black Migration in the 1950s

Although the migrations of the 1940s were caused in large part by the attraction of economic opportunity, this was not true of the

Study of Negro Life in a Northern City, rev. and enlarged ed. (New York: Harcourt Brace 1962), 2 vols.; and Horace Clark, Dark Ghetto: Dilemmas of Social Power (New York: Harper & Row, 1965). The relationship of ghettoization to the black migration is analyzed in Gilbert Osofsky, Harlem: The Making of a Ghetto (New York: Harper & Row, 1965), and Allan H. Spear, Black Chicago: The Making of a Negro Ghetto, 1890-1920 (Chicago: University of Chicago Press, 1967). One of the few studies of blacks in northern cities prior to the migrations is W. E. B. DuBois, The Philadelphia Negro: A Social Study (New York: Schocken Books, 1967), which was first published in 1899.

migrations of the 1950s. They were the result largely of the transformation of southern agriculture, and for some five years their pace exceeded anything that had gone before. Between 1950 and 1960 some 1,500,000 blacks moved to the North. Most of this migration took place before 1957, and for the first part of the 1950s its pace was apparently double that of even the 1940s. Machinery displaced men on a large scale in the most backward areas of the rural South, and the northward stream of black migrants engulfed the inner cities of the North and Midwest.

By 1960 the distribution of the nation's black population had shifted drastically. As late as 1920 it was largely southern rural (64 percent). Forty years later it was heavily urban (74 percent), and more than half (54 percent) of all urban blacks lived outside the South. Table 2.1 shows the data in more detail.

The population structure of northern cities was radically transformed by the black migration of the 1950s. Figure 2.1 shows the changes that took place in Detroit between 1950 and 1960. Whites moved out in large numbers, particularly in the 20 to 40 age group that took many young children with them. The only white age group that increased significantly in numbers was the over 65 group. The

TABLE 2.1

Regional and Urban-Rural Distribution of the Black Population, 1920 and 1960
(Millions of Persons)

RESIDENCE	1920	1960
South—rural	6,661,000	4,704,000
urban	2,251,000	6,608,000
Total	8,912,000	11,312,000
Percent urban	25.3	58.4
North and West—rural	242,000	355,000
urban	1,258,000	7,193,000
Total	1,500,000	7,548,000
Percent urban	83.8	95.3
Total black population	10,412,000	18,505,000

SOURCE: C. Horace Hamilton, "The Negro Leaves the South," *Demography,* Vol. 1, No. 1 (1964), p. 276.

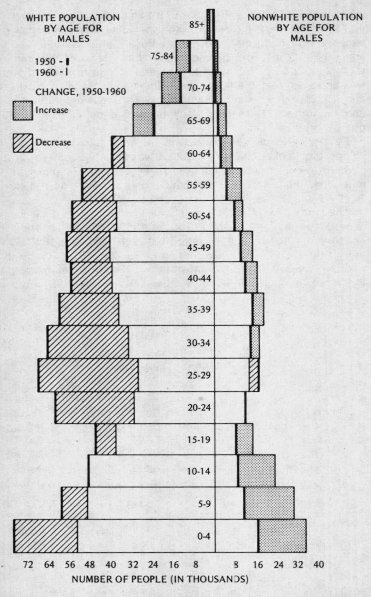

FIGURE 2.1   Changes in the Population Structure of Detroit, 1950-1960

black population grew, but the largest increases were the ages under 20 years. Indeed, there was a small decline in the 20 to 29 age group.

Economic Conditions in the Northern Cities

The migrants of the 1950s found a different situation in the North than did their counterparts of earlier periods. There were few jobs available for them when they got to the northern cities. The reasons were chiefly to be found in structural difficulties in the labor market and in national economic trends.[4]

First, the southern refugees of the 1950s were among the least skilled and worst educated of all Americans. The skills that they had were largely agricultural. What education they had was obtained in rural southern schools not known for their quality. There was not much that they could do that businessmen wanted now that cost-plus wartime production was ended.

Second, the mass production industries of the northern cities were not hiring. There were two chief reasons for this situation. One was automation, then being applied on a large scale in such industries as automobiles, steel, and electrical equipment, which enabled the mass production industries to expand output without increasing their work force. In automobiles, for example, the work force was actually reduced during the 1950s while output rose. Yet it was in these industries primarily that unskilled and semiskilled jobs had been found by the earlier black migrants of the 1940s.[5]

Third, national economic growth slowed down. The nation's GNP increased at a rate of only 2.4 percent annually between 1953 and 1960, as compared with 4 percent per year from 1946 to 1953. Unemployment rose throughout the economy, and a substantial amount of economic slack developed. Under these conditions the uneducated black migrant was not only the last to be hired, but in many instances he was not hired at all.

Fourth, black migrants from the South faced competition in the labor market from whites displaced from northern farms. Technolog-

[4]The following discussion of the causes of high rates of unempolyment for blacks in the 1950s and 1960s draws heavily on Charles Killingsworth, *Jobs and Incomes for Negroes* (Ann Arbor; Institute of Labor and Industrial Relations, University of Michigan, 1968).

[5]According to M. T. Puryear, "Automation and technological change tend to create the greatest displacements in those occupational classifications where the bulk of the Negro labor force is concentrated." M. T. Puryear, "Technology and the Negro," in *Adjusting to Change*, Appendix, Vol. III, *Technology and the American Economy*, Report of the National Commission on Technology, Automation, and Economic Progress (Washington: U. S. Government Printing Office, 1966), pp. 131.

ical transformation in U.S. agriculture has been a national phenomenon, particularly in the 25 years after 1940. When the decline in farm employment began in 1920, some 11.5 million persons were employed in agriculture. By 1940 the figure had fallen to 9.5 million, but by 1964 it had dropped to 4.7 million, or about half the level of the last pre-World War II year.[6] The white workers released from agriculture moved into urban areas, too. Since they were better educated and more highly skilled than the southern black migrants, and were not black, they tended to get the available jobs.

Fifth, what economic expansion there was took place on the fringes of the metropolitan areas. Factories were being built in suburban industrial parks. New plants were set down in open fields. In large part jobs in the new locations were unavailable to the black migrants, who settled mainly in the central cities. Development of lily-white suburbs kept blacks from residences within easy reach of the new plants. In addition, public transportation systems were seriously deteriorating in the 1950s and were not extended to the new industrial areas, and access to suburban jobs was difficult.

The Economic Shift to the Suburbs

The decentralization of employment was particularly strong in the 1950s, coinciding with the large increase in the black population of the central cities. Between 1954 and 1958, according to a study made by John F. Kain, employment in central cities grew very slowly, while jobs were expanding rapidly in the suburban ring. Of 40 central cities, 30 showed a decline in manufacturing employment, 18 in wholesale trade, 17 in retail trade, and 4 in service employment.[7] The overall picture from Kain's data is shown in Table 2.2.

The situation in New York City was typical. Employment opportunities were growing on Long Island, in Westchester County, and in northern New Jersey. But blacks with few exceptions could not buy houses in the new suburban developments. Tremendous public investments were made in building high-speed expressways to serve the newly opened areas, but the city subways were not extended,

[6]See Walter R. Butcher, "Productivity, Technology and Employment in U. S. Agriculture," in The Employment Impact of Technology Change, Appendix, Vol. II, Technology and the American Economy, Report of the National Commission on Technology, Automation, and Economic Progress (Washington: U. S. Government Printing Office, 1966), pp. 135-152.

[7]John F. Kain, "The Distribution and Movement of Jobs in Industry," in John Q. Wilson (ed.), The Metropolitan Enigma (Washington: U. S. Chamber of Commerce, 1967), p. 14.

TABLE 2.2

Percent Changes in Employment in 40 United States Metropolitan Areas, 1954-1958

| | ANNUAL PERCENT CHANGE IN EMPLOYMENT | |
	CENTRAL CITIES	SUBURBAN RING
Manufacturing	- 1.7	7.4
Wholesale trade [a]	0.2	16.6
Retail trade	0.1	13.5
Services	3.9	17.0

[a]For thirty-nine metropolitan areas only.

SOURCE: John F. Kain, "The Distribution and Movement of Jobs and Industry," in J. Q. Wilson (ed.), *The Metropolitan Enigma* (Washington: U. S. Chamber of Commerce, 1967), p. 11.

and service on the expensive commuter railroads became progressively worse at higher rates. Even the expressways were of little use to the man in the black ghetto: he had no car, or the money to buy one. Even if he did, there was no place to keep it in Harlem or Bedford-Stuyvesant. The available jobs might just as well have been in Timbuktu.[8]

Programs designed to aid the cities only made the problem worse. Billions of dollars were poured into construction of expressways and urban development. As far as blacks were concerned, everyone else benefited. Housing was demolished to create empty city blocks, and when replaced, the new housing was usually for upper-and middle-income groups. Worse yet, areas were marked out for redevelop-

[8]There is some debate over the significance of transportation problems as a cause of unemployment of blacks. A study at the Survey Research Center at the University of Michigan indicates that people who live in the central city travel furthest, spend the most time, and have the highest transportation costs in getting to their jobs. These are also among the poorest groups in the population and can least afford the higher costs. James N. Morgan, "A Note on the Time Spent on the Journey to Work," *Demography*, Vol. 4, No. 1 (1967), pp. 360-362.

On the other hand, another study has raised some questions about whether patterns of housing segregation have significantly reduced employment opportunities for residents of central cities. See John F. Kain, "Housing Segregation, Negro Employment, and Metropolitan Decentralization," *Quarterly Journal of Economics*, Vol. LXXXII, No. 2 (May 1968), pp. 175-197. Kain's data have been retested by Donald Deskins, who has shown that Kain's conclusions were probably correct for the period he studied (the mid-1950s) but were no longer true for the mid-1960s, by which time the patterns of housing segregation and decentralization of jobs were a significant cause of black unemployment. See Donald R. Deskins, "Residence-Workplace Interaction Vectors for the Detroit Metropolitan Area," Special Publication No. 3, Department of Geography, Northwestern University (Evanston, 1970), pp. 1-23.

ment or expressway construction three, five, and even ten years ahead of time, with the result that existing housing was allowed by its owners to deteriorate. Invariably, these sites were primarily the areas where the poor resided. In addition, failure to act promptly on construction projects helped to create slums by fostering deterioration and overcrowding. The suburbanite, the merchant, and the land developer got the benefits, while the black ghetto was squeezed.[9]

The Population Explosion and It's Impact

On top of all this came a population explosion of severe proportions. The black migrants were young and the women of child-bearing age. They had come from a rural society with a traditionally high birth rate and large families—and from areas with the highest maternal and infant mortality rates in the country. When they moved north, both the infant and maternal mortality rates fell (even though they remain high in comparison with those of the white suburbs). This combination of factors—large numbers of uprooted young people, traditions of large families, and higher survival rates—created rapid rates of population growth. The scope of this population explosion has been little studied, and exact statistics are hard to find. But it is reflected in the national rates of population growth: between 1950 and 1960 the white population of the United States increased by 17.6 percent, while the black population grew almost 50 percent faster—by 25.4 percent.

The central city population explosion put tremendous pressure on the cities. Population densities in the urban ghettos rose. As the slums became blacker and burst their boundaries, middle-income whites moved to the suburbs. This process substituted low-income for middle-income taxpayers in the cities, property values deteriorated, and the urban tax base withered. At the same time larger numbers of people who needed increased services had to be provided for. A sudden growth in needs was accompanied by a corresponding drop in resources. The result was a serious deterioration of public services in such crucial areas as health, police and fire protection and education. The urban financial crisis escalated.[10]

[9] See James Q. Wilson (ed.), *Urban Renewal: The Record and the Controversy* (Cambridge, M.I.T. Press, 1966); Scott Greer, *Urban Renewal and American Cities* (Indianapolis, Bobbs-Merrill, 1965); and Martin Anderson, *The Federal Bulldozer* (Cambridge, Mass: M.I.T. Press, 1964 and New York: McGraw-Hill, 1967).

[10] There is a surprising lack of documentation of the urban financial crisis, although it is much discussed and commented upon. Data on its extent and severity are lacking.

Two pioneering studies of the public finance problems of metropolitan areas are Harvey E. Brazer, "The Role of Major Metropolitan Centers in State and Local Finance,"

Education, in particular, has suffered. For example, in the census area of which riot-torn Twelfth Street in Detroit is a part, the number of families and unrelated individuals counted by the census fell by about 4,700 between 1950 and 1965. But the number of children of school age increased by 20,900 in the same period. Even with all the good will in the world, in the absence of vastly increased resources the school authorities could do little but watch the quality of education decline. Unable to provide the funds needed, school officials have presided over the breakdown of the educational systems of the central cities. The people who needed the best got the worst.[11]

The extent of the breakdown of the urban educational system is only now being documented in detail. A 1970 study[12] of big city high schools prepared for the National Association of Secondary School Principals showed that schools with high-quality academic standards migrated to the suburbs with the upper middle-income families. Central city high schools had to deal with large numbers of "young people who do poorly in school and who do not get jobs or make satisfactory adult adjustments when they drop out of school." To the low expectation for students was added a lack of teachers with the experience required to cope with the influx of a new kind of student, administrators often too rigid to change their ideals from those appropriate to a high-quality upper-middle-income student to a high-quality low-income student, and a general shortage of funds as the number of students rose as rapidly as the tax base fell.

American Economic Review, Vol. XLVIII, No. 2 (May 1958), pp. 305–316, and William J. Baumol, "Interactions of Public and Private Decisions," in Howard G. Schaller (ed.), *Public Expenditure Decisions in the Urban Community* (Washington: Resources for the Future, 1963).

One of the few studies to document the decline of the tax base because of the decline of property values is Chester Rapkin, *The Real Estate Market in an Urban Renewal Area* (New York: New York City Planning Commission, 1959). Rapkin also documents the almost complete ending of new construction in the affected areas, the termination of institutional mortgage flows, the acquisition of property by the absentee "slumlord" investor, and the shift to furnished-room occupancy.

Perhaps the best overview of the urban financial crisis is to be found in Advisory Commission on Intergovernmental Relations, *Urban America and the Federal System* (Washington: U. S. Government Printing Office, 1969), esp. Ch. 2.

[11]The key study of the problem is Patricia Sexton, *Education and Income* (New York: Viking Press, 1961). Some impressionistic accounts are Bel Kaufman, *Up the Down Staircase* (New York, Prentice-Hall, 1964); Jonathan Kozol, *Death At an Early Age* (Boston: Houghton Mifflin, 1967): and Herbert Kohl, *Thirty-Six Children* (New York: New American Library, 1968). See also the early study by James B. Conant, *Slums and Suburbs* (New York, McGraw-Hill, 1961), and the recent Christopher Jencks, *Inequality: A Reassessment of the Effect of Family and Schooling in America* (New York: Basic Books, 1972).

[12]Robert J. Havighurst, Frank L. Smith, Jr., and David E. Wilder, "A Profile of the Large City High School" (Washington: National Association of Secondary School Principals, 1970).

The failure of urban educational systems was particularly important. The huge migration of young blacks came in the early 1950s, and the inner city population explosion followed. The children, badly educated in deteriorating school systems, were poorly fitted with the skills needed by the modern labor market. What skills they had were more suited to survival in the jungle of the central cities than in the industrial plants of the metropolitan fringe. It was these young people who hit the labor markets in large numbers in the mid- and late 1960s, only to find few opportunities.

Unemployment rates in the urban ghettos were two to three times the unemployment rates of metropolitan areas in the mid-1960s. If a metropolitan area had an overall unemployment rate of 4 percent, we could expect a ghetto unemployment rate of 8 to 12 percent.

Even worse were the subemployment rates, a new measure of employment developed by the U. S. Department of Labor.[13] In addition to regularly measured unemployment, it includes the part-time employed who are seeking full-time employment, full-time workers earning less than a poverty level income, and persons of working age who dropped out of the labor market through discouragement. In 1966 (the only year for which data has been published) subemployment rates in ten urban ghettos ranged between 24 and 47 percent. These figures showed a disastrous situation: one-quarter to one-half of the ghetto labor force was "subemployed."

These were the circumstances surrounding the revolt of the urban ghetto in the middle and late 1960s. The urban ghettos, with a population heavily concentrated in low-wage, unskilled or semiskilled, and service employment, suffering from racial discrimination in housing and the labor market, were struck by a great migration and population explosion that brought serious deterioration in the social fabric, in social controls, and in public services. By the mid-1960s the employment situation was catastrophic. And racial attitudes on the part of whites promised no hope for any improvement. In retrospect, the explosion seems to have been the most natural thing in the world. One wonders why it was so long in coming.

---

[13]See "A Sharper Look at Unemployment in the U. S. Cities and Slums," and studies of subemployment in the slums of various cities, U. S. Department of Labor, Washington, D. C., n.d. The U. S. Senate Subcommittee on Employment, Manpower, and Poverty has extended the analysis of subemployment to show that in 1970 up to 60 percent of the inner city work force does not earn enough to maintain a decent standard of living and 30 percent did not earn even a poverty-level income. See William Spring, Bennett Harrison, and Thomas Vietorisz, "Crisis of the Underemployed," New York Times Magazine, Nov. 5, 1972, pp. 42ff.

CHAPTER 3

The Ghetto Economy: Work and Wages

The ghetto economy is a world apart. It differs markedly from that of the rest of the country in many ways. Perhaps its most important distinguishing characteristic is its backwardness. It lacks the dynamic, progressive changes that bring advancement to the rest of the economy. Although there are points of contact through which the ghetto is influenced by economic activity in the rest of the nation, its economy has many of the characteristics of a partial enclave that is only incompletely articulated with the world outside.

Sources of Income

The income of the urban poverty area comes from four major sources, only one of which represents a viable and continuing link with the forces of progress.

1. The high-wage, progressive sectors of the economy provide employment for same residents. In Detroit, for example, jobs in the automobile industry are held by a racially integrated work force, a number of whose members live in the urban ghettos. The industry is highly capital-intensive and oligopolistic and has a strong union; labor productivity is high and wages correspond. Detroit, however, is an exception in regard to the percentage of its ghetto residents who work in a high-wage industry. Most large cities have a much smaller portion of their central city work force in such industries.

2. The chief economic base of the urban poverty area is the more backward sector of the economy, characterized by low wages, relatively wide cyclical variations, and exposure to all the debilitating forces of competition. A large portion of the workers who are employed full time in these industries earn wages around or below the poverty level.

3. The low-wage economy is supplemented by an "irregular" economy, partly legal and partly illegal, which provides further income for the residents of urban poverty areas, argely through provision of services to other residents.

4. Income supplements from outside the urban poverty areas, some public and some private, provide the transfer payments without which the population could not survive. Welfare payments are proba-

bly the largest and certainly the most controversial of these transfers.

Although these four aspects of the economy of urban poverty areas can be relatively easily identified, the studies which would document their extent and significance have not been made. We do not know, for example, the proportion of the income of residents generated by these sources. Nor do we know which are increasing and which are decreasing. Nor do we have much notion of how the four sectors have changed in recent years. Nevertheless, it is possible to look more closely at several of them.

The Low-wage Industries and the Working Poor

A large number of ghetto residents work in low-wage industries. The jobs may be in manufacturing, service industries, or retail and wholesale trade. Their common characteristic is that many full-time employees who work steadily in these industries earn less than a poverty-level income. Table 3.1 gives some examples of industries in which a large proportion of all employees fall in the category of the working poor.[1]

The preponderance of low-wage employment in the ghettos is shown by data for central Harlem from the U. S. Department of Labor's 1966 study of *Sub-Employment in the Slums of New York.* Median family income was $3,907 as compared with $6,300 for the U.S. as a whole. The distribution of occupations, shown in Table 3.2, demonstrates a heavy preponderance of low-skilled and low-wage occupations.

The survey did not break down the white-collar occupations into the two classifications of professional-managerial (mostly high wage) and clerical-sales (mostly low wage). An educated guess would allocate 20 percent of the white-collar employment, at the most, to the former category and 80 percent to the latter. Adding in the low-wage laborers and service workers would lead to the division between low-and high-wage employment shown in Table 3.3. The calculation in the table is an estimate, of course, and is derived from only one central city ghetto, although one of the largest. A rough

[1]This discussion of low-wage employment is based in large part upon Barry Bluestone, "Low Wage Industries and the Working Poor," *Poverty and Human Resources Abstracts*, Vol. III, No. 2 (March-April 1968), pp. 1-13. See also Dawn Wachtel, "The Working Poor," Institute of Labor and Industrial Relations, University of Michigan (mimeo, 1967), and Harold L. Sheppard, *The Nature of the Job Problem and the Role of New Public Service Employment* (Kalamazoo, Michigan, Upjohn Institute for Employment Research, 1969), pp. 2-11.

TABLE 3.1

Selected Low-wage Industries Employing Substantial Numbers of the Urban Poor

INDUSTRY	YEAR	TOTAL EMPLOYMENT	AVERAGE HOURLY EARNINGS	% EARNINGS LESS THAN $1.60/HR.
Nursing homes and related facilities	1965	172,637	$1.19	86.3
Laundries and cleaning services	1966	397,715	1.44	72.5
Hospitals (excl. federal)	1966	1,781,300	1.86	41.2
Work clothing	1964	57,669	1.43	72.8
Men's and boy's shirts	1964	96,935	1.45	70.4
Candy and other confectionery	1965	49,736	1.87	34.2
Limited price variety stores	1965	277,100	1.31	87.9
Eating and drinking places	1963	1,286,708	1.14	79.4
Hotels and motels	1963	416,289	1.17	76.1
Department stores	1965	1,019,300	1.75	59.6
Miscellaneous retail stores	1965	968,200	1.75	58.0
Retail food stores	1965	1,366,800	1.91	47.6

SOURCE: Adapted from Barry Bluestone, "Low Wage Industries and the Working Poor," *Poverty and Human Resources Abstracts*, Vol. III, No. 2 (March–April 1968), Supplement, pp. 6–7.

TABLE 3.2

**Occupations of Employed Persons, Central Harlem,
November 1966**

OCCUPATION	NUMBER	PERCENT OF TOTAL
White-collar	21,272	27.5
Blue-collar		
Craftsmen	4,642	6.0
Operatives	13,398	17.3
Laborers	11,718	15.1
Service	26,460	34.1
Total	77,490	100.0

approximation of about 70 percent of all ghetto employed working in the low-wage sector is consistent with other general descriptions. One would not be surprised if the figure were as high as 75 percent, but would be surprised if it were lower than two-thirds.

The low-wage industries are not highly visible, and we do not look to them for examples of progress. Typically, the individual enterprise is small, requiring relatively little capital investment. The technology is labor-intensive. Both labor productivity and profits are low. Workers are subject to the wage squeeze characteristic of labor-intensive, highly competitive industries. Sales in these industries are generally quite sensitive to prices, which means that even if competition were reduced, firms would have little chance of improving their revenues through price increases. Since profits are low, little is

TABLE 3.3

**Estimated Low-Wage and High-Wage Employment
Central Harlem, November 1966**

	NUMBER	PERCENT OF TOTAL
Low-wage employment	55,196	71.2
High-wage employment	22,294	28.8
Total	77,490	100.0

done in research or product development, which reinforces the technological backwardness of the industry.

The low-wage industries may well be subject to greater fluctuations than other sectors of the economy when aggregate demand falls. We know that labor turnover rates are high, which means that the incidence of unemployment in the labor force is also high. We also know that the bulk of the work force is relatively poorly educated and has relatively low levels of work skills. Finally, a large proportion of the jobs are dead ends: there are not many higher paying jobs that a worker can qualify for by his daily work on the job. There are relatively few ladders to better positions. Workers who start out in the low wage sector of the economy apparently tend to stay there rather than move into similar jobs in the high-wage sector (although more studies of this phenomenon are needed to determine how strong a tendency this is).

These industries are part of the "unprotected" economy. For the most part, workers are not unionized. Employers are not protected by the oligopolistic industrial structure which shields such firms as General Motors Corp. and other industrial giants. Most protective legislation, such as minimum wage laws, is only now being extended to low-wage jobs, and a large number are still not covered. Many federal programs which might have provided greater protection, such as the loan operations of the Small Business Administration, are only beginning to provide services. Workers are exposed to the "satanic mills" of supply and demand, which grind both workers and business firms mighty fine. The higher income sectors of society have been protected while those needing it the most have gone exposed.

The low-wage labor force of the ghetto is preserved and reinforced by high rates of unemployment there. During the recession of 1970-1971, when national unemployment rates rose to levels of 6 to 7 percent of the labor force, unemployment rates in the inner city ghettos were doubled, reaching to 12 to 15 percent as measured by the U. S. Department of Labor. Even these official rates were deceptively low, because in the compilations for the 1965-1967 period the department had changed its definition of unemployed to exclude some who would be officially counted as out of work under the older method of estimating the unemployment rate. The employment picture for young people in the ghettos was far worse, with unemployment rates rising to 30 to 40 percent for persons under 21 years of age. The presence of these cadres of unemployed workers tends to keep wages low in those sectors of the labor market in which they compete. These are the low-wage industries and the menial occupations for which racial minorities are elgible.

Lack of union organization is another element that reinforces the low-wage pattern. The high-wage industries are largely unionized, and unions offer some degree of insulation against the pressures of supply and demand in the labor market. When a firm has a union contract that embodies an agreement on wages, the management has little to gain from replacing existing employees with new men, for the new men will have to be paid at the same wage rates as the old. Even during recessions most unions are able effectively to resist wage cuts, and many are able to achieve increases based on productivity gains. Workers in the ghettos are less fortunate. Unemployment rates there are always high—double the national level even in the best of times—and wage rates are held down by the ability of the employer to replace workers at any time. There are few unions to protect the low-wage worker from the impact of the market.

The presence of a large labor force employed in low-wage industries is of major significance to the larger metropolitan regions of which the ghettos are a part. The industries of any metropolitan area can be divided into three groups. One group comprises the "export" industries that provide the *raison d'etre* for the regional economy. They are oriented toward national (and international) markets, like automobiles in Detroit or steel in Pittsburgh, to cite two classic examples. A second group is complementary to the first. These industries provide inputs for use by the "export" industries or use their outputs for further processing. Both groups, generally, are characterized by large firms, pay high wages, use modern technology, and are unionized in most parts of the country. The third group of industries supply the local economy with food, clothing, shelter, medical care, education, recreation, governmental services, and the like. Many are low-wage industries, and it is in this sector that most ghetto residents are normally employed.[2]

An inherently exploitive relationship is established. Living costs in the whole metropolitan area are held down by the existence of low-wage service industries. Costs of production in the export industries and their complementary firms are lower because the services they buy are, in part, provided by a low-wage work force. All of the

[2]This classification follows that of Stanislaw Czamanski, "A Model of Urban Growth," *Papers of the Regional Science Association* (1964), pp. 177-200, and "A Method of Forecasting Regional Growth by Means of Distributed Lag Analysis," *Journal of Regional Science,* Vol. 6 No. 1 (Summer 1965), pp. 35-49.

products and services on which the life of the community are based are available at prices that reflect the low wages paid to ghetto residents.[3]

This economic relationship makes it difficult for any local government to take strong action to eliminate ghettos and the poverty found there. If one area made a serious effort along those lines, there would be an increase in the cost base of the area's export industries and their complements. Services would cost more, the cost of distribution would be higher, and governmental expenses would rise. Higher living costs would require higher wages in the export and complementary industries in order to attract and keep the necessary amounts of properly skilled labor. These higher costs (relative to other metropolitan areas) would result in slower economic growth and perhaps even retrogression if the cost effects were great enough. Low wages in service industries are as important to a city's export industries as are low taxes.

Admittedly, these effects would be felt in the form of marginal changes, but they would be pervasive and persistent. They would be felt particularly by real estate and commercial interests, whose stake in local economic growth is greatest and who normally are influential in determining local governmental policies. It is in their interest, and in the interest of other elements in the local power structure, that the area should come last with the least effort to ameliorate or end the poverty inherent in low-wage industries.

There is a similar economic interest on the part of middle-income groups. If wages are raised in the low-wage industries, the cost of living will rise and their standard of living will fall. Many people are aware of this relationship, although it is usually expressed in some phrase such as, "Someone has to wash the dishes," or "Who will collect the trash?"

The basically exploitive nature of the urban ghetto is readily evident. It is easy to understand why there are strong economic and political barriers to its elimination. The structure of power is allied with those economic interests that have a vested interest in continued poverty. Unfortunately, those economic interests constitute a majority of those who vote.

---

[3]Local patterns of economic growth are also affected by wage rates in the export and complementary industries, but those wage rates are heavily influenced by national patterns of collective bargaining and tend to be relatively uniform between urban areas.

The Irregular Economy[4]

The urban ghetto supports an occupational structure and service economy that is quite unconventional and partly illegitimate. The need for it arises from the inability of residents to pay for the usual organized and commercially provided services used by higher income areas and from the lack of business enterprises which normally provide them. To compensate for this lack, the ghetto economy has developed an "irregular" economy which involves (1) informal work patterns that are often invisible to outside observers, (2) a network of occupational skills unique to ghetto life but which have little significance for jobs outside the ghetto, and (3) acquisition of skills and competences by workers in nontraditional ways, making their use in the larger society difficult if not impossible.

Louis Ferman has identified several occupational types in the irregular economy:

> *The artist.* Entertainers, humorists, painters, and craftsmen.
> *The hustler.* The supersalesman who often operates on both sides of the law: for example, the "casket salesman" who retrieves coffins from the local cemetery, refubishes them, and offers them for sale.
> *The fixer.* The expert who can repair cars, appliances, plumbing, or electrical wiring.
> *The information broker.* The individual who receives cash income in exchange for information. Sometimes the information concerns the availability of stolen merchandise, sometimes job opportunities, sometimes the details of the welfare system.
> *The product developer.* Products such as rum-raisin ice cream, sweet potato pie, and barbecued spareribs enjoy large sale in some ghettos. They are also produced there for sale by ghetto residents.

[4]This section is based on Louis A. Ferman, "The Irregular Economy: Informal Work Patterns in the Urban Ghetto," Institute of Labor and Industrial Relations, University of Michigan (mimeo, n.d). See also Michael J. Piore, "Public and Private Responsibilities in On-the-Job Training of Disadvantaged Workers," Department of Economics Working Paper No. 23, Department of Economics, Massachusetts Institute of Technology (mimeo, 1968). Descriptions of life styles based on the irregular economy can be found in Elliott Liebow, *Tally's Corner, A Study of Street-Corner Men* (Boston: Little, Brown, 1967); Claude Brown, *Manchild in the Promised Land* (New York: Macmillan, 1965); Oscar Lewis, *La Vida* (New York: Random House, 1965); Peri Thomas: *Down These Mean Streets* (New York: Knopf, 1967); Malcolm X, *Autobiography* (New York: Grove Press, 1965); and Herbert Gans, *The Urban Villagers* (New York: Free Press, 1962).

Some of these irregular occupations are practiced full time, some part time, some almost as hobbies. They all fill needs not served through regular economic channels. Most are not illegal, although there is a substantial amount of illegal activity as well carried out by fences, thieves, bookies, narcotics pushers, pimps, and prostitutes.

Since there have been no systematic studies of the irregular economy, little is known about how closely people are tied to it or whether they move back and forth between the irregular and the regular work systems.Ferman noted five typical situations.

The worker holds a steady job in the regular economy but moonlights in the irregular economy to earn more, using the same skills used on his regular job.

The worker is sporadically employed in the regular economy (which he considers his chief employment) but works in the irregular economy when unemployed.

The worker shifts back and forth between the regular and irregular economies, depending on where he finds the best opportunities.

The worker is employed primarily in the irregular economy but ventures occasionally into a regular job.

The worker is wholly employed in the irregular economy and never works in a regular job.

The irregular economy has certain advantages over work in the regular economy. The worker is not accountable to any authority for his earnings, no records are kept, and taxes can be avoided. The work is individualistic in nature and can give the worker a sense of competence and control over his existence that a regular job may not provide. Entrepreneurship and risk give the activity some of the aspects of a game, yet the risks are usually not high. Finally, people who work either part or full time in the regular economy can supplement their incomes in the irregular economy, and vice versa.

The irregular economy has one major disadvantage, however. It encourages patterns of behavior and attitudes toward work which make it difficult for a worker accustomed to the irregularity, lax work standards, and high rates of labor turnover in the irregular economy to move easily into jobs in the regular economy, where work rules are more rigid, lost time and absenteeism is not tolerated to the same extent, and supervision is more rigorous. In some respects the work habits of the irregular economy are similar to those of the pre-industrial work force that economic historians are familiar with, and some of the same difficulties are found in adapting workers in the irregular economy to jobs in the mainstream of a modern industrial society.

However, the irregular economy does enable people to develop productive skills, entrepreneurship, and sales ability that could be developed and put to use in more systematic ways for the economic development of the area. Its very existence indicates an unfortunate waste of ability and intelligence. Although the specific skills of the irregular economy may not be highly applicable in the regular economy, they indicate the presence of a high degree of initiative and entrepreneurship.

Crime in the Ghetto[5]

The ghetto is the home of organized crime that continually bleeds the poor of hundreds of millions of dollars annually. Four criminal industries are particularly important: numbers, loan sharking, drugs, and prostitution. They comprise the bulk of that portion of the irregular economy outside the law.

The most lucrative is the numbers racket, or policy game. It is a form of gambling in which an individual bets on a three-digit number, with the winning number being selected by chance—for example, the last three digits of the day's parimutuel receipts at a major racetrack. The payoff is very large, but the odds against winning are even larger. The operator does not have to be dishonest to have large earnings as long as the odds are fixed at the proper level.

A very large proportion of slum residents play the policy game. The New York State Joint Legislative Committee on Crime estimated that in 1968 it was played by 75 percent of all adult and late teenage slum residents in New York City, who spend an average of $3 to $5 a week on it. In the three ghetto areas of Harlem, South Bronx, and Bedford-Stuyvesant some $150 million is spent on it annually, according to estimates made by city and state officials.

[5]On crime in the ghetto, see a series of articles in the New York Times, "Cubans Here Are Ending Mafia's Monopoly of Numbers Racket," Feb. 22, 1970, p. 36; "Heroin Traffickers Here Tell How $219 Million Trade Works," Apr. 20, 1970, pp. 1, 36; "Organized Crime in City Robs Black Slums of Millions, " Sept. 27, 1970, pp. 1, 85; "Numbers Called Harlem's Balm," Mar. 1, 1971, pp. 1, 44; and Fred J. Cook, "The Black Mafia Moves into the Numbers Racket," New York Times Magazine, Apr. 4, 1971, pp. 26ff. The Reports of the New York State Legislative Committee on Crime provide a great deal of information on organized crime in the urban ghettos. Although these references primarily pertain to the New York City ghettos, the situation is similar in the ghettos of other major cities.

In order to operate the numbers racket, a network of organized crime permeates the entire ghetto. Hundreds of "runners" fan out into houses, apartments, stores, and factories to collect bets. The runners bring the bets and records to "controllers," usually store owners, who collect the money, record the bets, and send the information to the "bank" or "office" via runners or pickup men. The controller usually receives 35 percent of the bets brought in by his runners, who are usually paid a salary. The numbers banker gets the rest, out of which comes the day's payoff to winners. The controller is usually responsible for expenses, such as bail and legal fees for the participants who are arrested "in the line of duty," and payoffs to police. The overall profit margin of a numbers network is about 25 percent, after all costs. Most of the money does not stay in the ghetto. Although some of the runners and controllers may be residents of the ghetto, the men at the top generally are not. In New York City, for example, the numbers game employs many blacks and Puerto Ricans, but the top management is alleged to be the Mafia— a number of whom have been driven from the city by the police and operate through lieutenants as absentee lords of the racket.

Loan sharking is closely associated with numbers gambling. The numbers bank is a source of funds, and the network of runners provides a means of communication. There is also a network of loan sharks who haunt the street corners, stores, and work places. Small loans are made at interest rates that range upward to 20 percent a week. Once a loan is made—usually for $10 to $25—little pressure to repay is exercised as long as the interest is paid regularly. Ghetto residents are at the mercy of this system, for many of them need money before payday or the arrival of the welfare check. Their resources are often meager, and there are no other sources of loans. Lenders do not fear betrayal to the police because their customers have no other place to turn in emergencies.

Narcotics is a much smaller but far more profitable segment of the criminal underworld. Based on estimates made by the New York State Joint Legislative Committee on Crime, the three major slum areas of New York City had between 12,000 and 24,000 drug addicts in 1968. The number has probably increased substantially since, for there has been a major increase in drug use in the years since the black revolt of the mid-1960s. The average addict needs about $30 a day for drugs, or about $10,000 a year. This would bring the gross revenue of the narcotics business in the three major ghettos to between $120 million and $250 million annually in 1968. Recent increases have greatly increased the figures.

It is believed that the business is controlled by the Mafiosi to an even greater extent than are numbers and loan sharking. With greatly intensified law enforcement drives against the traffic in drugs, however, the more risky parts of the business—inporting and distribution—have been increasingly turned over to blacks, Puerto Ricans, and Latin Americans eager for the high profits that can be obtained. Control, financing, and the bulk of the gains have remained with the established gangland structure.

Narcotics is the source of two other complementary industries, prostitution and the distribution of stolen goods. The narcotics addict must have a steady source of large income. Unless he is part of the business itself, there is little opportunity to earn the money needed. Girls and women turn to prostitution and men and boys to stealing. Both provide the base for industries in which the workers earn enough to sustain their drug habit while others make large profits.

The traffic in stolen goods is large. Most of the business is carried on through fences, who normally pay 20 percent of the wholesale value of the goods: an addict who needs $10,000 a year to support his habit has to steal $50,000 worth of salable merchandise annually. On this basis the addicts of the three major New York City ghettos alone would have been responsible for theft of some $300 to $500 million in 1968 if half of the cost of their drug habit were financed by stealing.

The goods move into a nationwide distribution network. They are sold to legitimate business firms in all parts of the country at two to three times the cost to the fence, which is still only 40 to 60 percent of the normal wholesale price. Much of this wholesale trade is said to be in the hands of the Mafiosi and represents its "legitimate" face. Even some of the retail outlets that deal in stolen goods at second or third hand have, it is believed, come under Mafiosi control.

The ghettos suffer most of all. Most of the narcotics addicts are slum-dwelling blacks or Puerto Ricans. They steal from nearby sources, preying on their own neighborhoods. Ghetto business enterprise suffers heavily. According to several studies, robberies of stores in central city commercial areas are twice as frequent as in the suburbs, and armed robberies during business hours are four times as frequent. Enterprises lose as a result, pay higher insurance costs (if insurance can be obtained) and pass on the higher costs to their customers. When special law enforcement and crime prevention programs are instituted in ghetto areas, the stealing is moved to surrounding parts of the city—which is the chief reason (rather than graft) that little is done about it. The political repercussions from nonghetto areas make a hands-off, containment policy the sensible thing for city governments to do.

Public opinion in the ghettos about the crime that preys upon the residents is mixed. On the one hand, there is strong sentiment for action against the narcotics traffic because of its subversion of the young and its connection with prostitution, stealing, and armed robbery. On the other hand, however, there is a good deal of admiration for the successful hustler, who has power and money and is able to meet the white nonghetto world on its own terms. This attitude is particularly strong among the young, for whom most other opportunities are highly restricted. In addition, the inability of law enforcement agencies to distinguish between criminals and ordinary citizens—the source of much of the "harassment" of which blacks and Puerto Ricans complain—makes many ghettoites leery of increased police action. Finally, the illegal industries permeate the lives of many ghettoites, providing important sources of excitement, entertainment, and emergency sources of funds. They are an integral part of a functioning economic system and will continue as long as the system remains.

A Separate World

The labor market of the inner city ghetto is an integral part of the economy of our urban areas. It provides a low-wage work force employed largely in the service industries to provides a low-cost base for any area's export industries and their complements and for the living standards of middle-and upper-income groups. The low-wage system is preserved by high levels of unemployment, which create continual pressures in the labor market to keep wages low.

The low-income population of the ghetto, in turn, supports an irregular economy that offers supplementary employment and income, but which functions in quite different ways from the economy outside the ghetto. The criminal industries are part of the irregular economy. By exploiting the ghetto they drain off resources and help keep the ghetto poor. Crime contributes to the preservation of the ghetto, and thereby to the presence of a reservoir of low-wage labor.

This view of the ghetto economy differs from the conventional theory of modern economics, which tends to view the labor market as a unified whole, as a seamless web of economic relationships in which all the parts are closely articulated. In that schema, low wages are the result of low productivity, and the poverty of the ghetto the result of low levels of education and skill. The fact that the ghettos are heavily black and Latin is attributed in large part to racial attitudes of employers. The "seamless web" theory of labor markets focuses not on structural deficiencies in the organization of the economy, but on elimination of discrimination and improvement of the poor.

The two following chapters present a different view of the matter. Chapter 4 develops the concept of the urban ghetto as an economic subsystem that is both part of the larger economy and at the same time separated from it. Resources and income drain into the larger economy to keep the ghetto underdeveloped and in a constant state of depression. At the same time the ghetto acts as a reservoir for the economic rejects of the progressive sector of the economy, while racial and other barriers make escape from the ghetto difficult. With this concept of the ghetto as a base, Chapter 5 examines the workings of a labor market in which minorities are crowded into menial occupations. It shows how the structure of labor markets lies behind the low wages and lack of opportunity that are associated with the ghetto economy. If the analysis in these chapters is correct, the ghetto is indeed a separate world structured in such a way as to create an exploited group of people whose prospects are permanent poverty and continued exploitation.

CHAPTER 4

The Economic Dynamics of the Ghetto

The urban ghetto is a depressed and underdeveloped enclave in the midst of a growing and progressive economy. A continuous drain of income and resources out of the ghetto keeps it in that condition. In that sense the ghetto is analagous to a colony. It is more than that, however. It is one of the places where rejects from the market economy—the human residuals of the economic system—come to rest. These two characteristics of the urban ghetto supplement its function as a source of low-wage labor to create a unique subsystem within the larger economic structure of modern society.

The Drain of Resources

One of the most striking characteristics of the urban poverty area is a continual drain of resources out of the area and into other sectors of the economy. The drain includes savings, physical capital, human resources, and incomes. As a result, urban poverty areas are left without the most important resources needed for development and improvement, and the economic infrastructure of supporting institutions is seriously deficient in those areas most necessary for improvement.

The drain of resources can be seen most clearly in the process of transition as an area becomes part of the spreading urban ghetto. As migration and population growth widen the boundaries of the ghetto into neighboring parts of the city, middle-class whites move out. With them go most of the professional personnel who provide personal and business services. Doctors, dentists, lawyers, and accountants, insurance agencies, and related professions leave and are not replaced.

Other human resources leave by way of the educational system and the high-wage economy. Drawn by opportunities outside the urban poverty area, many of the most intelligent, capable, and imaginative young people move into the progressive sectors where rewards are greater and opportunities are wider. This drain of human resources leaves the economy of the ghetto—whose chief resource is manpower—without many of its best products.

The drain of capital is equally striking. A substantial portion of the savings of the urban ghetto goes into financial institutions such as banks and savings banks whose investment policies draw the funds out of the area and into business loans, mortgages, and other investments elsewhere. Little comes back to support the ghetto economy or promote its development.[1] Even though the ownership of the original savings or thrift accounts remains with ghetto residents, the funds are generally used outside the ghetto.

Probably the largest flow of capital out of the urban poverty area, takes place in housing. Failure to maintain housing facilities enables the owner to withdraw his capital while he maintains his income. Ultimately, the property will be worthless simply because of wear and tear, but while it is being used up, the owner has been getting his capital back and has been deriving a nice current income. Housing authorities in most major cities are aware of this process but have found no way to stop it. Its basic causes lie in overcrowding and very high rates of deterioration through overuse, together with the failure of most cities to develop effective methods of preventing neighborhood decay.[2]

Two aspects of the drain in capital out of housing should be noted. If one or two property owners take their capital out by refusing to replace depreciation, in self-protection surrounding owners are forced to do likewise. One deteriorated building draws down the value of surrounding property. One house broken up into small apartments and crowded with numerous families makes it difficult to sell or rent to single families next door. These "neighborhood effects" cause the drain of capital to cumulate and accelerate once it begins and are almost impossible to stop.[3]

[1]Very little is known about the details of these money flows, and attempts have been made by several banks and insurance companies to redirect the flow of some of these funds back into the urban ghetto. We should also note that some ghetto savings are invested in rental housing by ghetto residents themselves. Studies are needed of the ownership of property in the urban poverty areas to obtain a better picture of these patterns. On the problems of black-owned banks, see Andrew J. Brimmer, "The Banking System and Urban Economic Development," a paper presented at the 1968 Annual Meeting of the American Real Estate and Urban Economics Association and the American Finance Association (mimeo, 1968).

[2]On the problems of slum housing, see Alvin L. Schorr, *Slums and Social Insecurity* (Washington: U. S. Department of Health, Education and Welfare, 1963), and Bernard J. Frieden, "Housing and National Urban Goals: Old Policies and New Realities," in *The Metropolitan Enigma* (Washington: U. S. Chamber of Commerce, 1967), pp. 148-191.

[3]See Chester Rapkin, *The Real Estate Market in an Urban Renewal Area* (New York: City Planning Commission, 1959), for a careful analysis and case study of the cumulative deterioration of housing. This process seems to have accelerated substantially in the early 1970s, particularly in the core area of large cities like New York, Philadelphia, Baltimore, Detroit, Chicago and St. Louis. On these developments, see "Federal Housing Abandonment Blights Inner Cities," *New York Times*, Jan. 13, 1972, pp. 1, 28.

In addition, families owning their own homes may find themselves locked into the ghetto because of income, age, or race. Their investment in property either deteriorates or its value rises much more slowly than that of families outside the ghetto. A white, suburban family discovers that economic growth creates a windfall gain in the form of rising property values. The effect on the ghetto family may be just the opposite: its house, located in a deteriorating urban ghetto, may well decline in value as the neighborhood deteriorates. At the very least, the ghetto resident owner discovers that over his lifetime the windfall gains from growth in property values is considerably below that of his white suburban counterpart.

Capital also flows out of urban poverty areas through public facilities. Local governments throughout the country have allowed their capital investments in poverty districts to fall by not replacing depreciation of buildings and other investments. Schools and libraries have been allowed to deteriorate, parks to run down, streets and curbs to go unrepaired, fire and police stations to depreciate, and medical facilities to deteriorate. In part, this process is due to the added strains that a denser population has placed on public facilities. In part, it is the result of the financial problems which prevented cities from increasing their expenditures for public services to meet expanding needs. However, in part, it is due to the traditional tendency of city governments to maintain facilities in the middle-and upper-income areas and to put the priorities of the slums last. Whatever the reasons, the lack of adequate government investment in the inner city results in another drain of capital out of urban poverty areas.

The transition to an urban ghetto also features the loss of many organized institutions. Hospitals move out. So do churches and other organized community groups. One of the striking characteristics of today's urban poverty area is a lack of those groups and associations which have traditionally provided a community with stability and order and with a sense of continuity and participation. This gap in social needs tends to be replaced by informal community groups. In the urban ghetto, however, much of this informal organization has been outside the law—juvenile gangs, for example. Lack of organized community groups, together with the strains inherent in poverty and the breakdown of family structures brought on by the system of welfare payments, contributes to and intensifies the isolation and anomie inherent in urban life. These social and psychological problems of the urban ghetto add a further dimension to the urban and racial crisis, but it is important to realize that they are related to the fundamental economic problems of the area and are not independent phenomena.

The Drain of Income

Income flows out of the urban poverty area in much the same way as capital and other resources. Earnings of residents are spent in stores owned outside the ghetto, and these same stores are very often staffed by employees from outside the ghetto. The earnings and profits of these outsiders are respent elsewhere and serve to promote economic growth elsewhere.

No community is self-sufficient. The goods purchased in any community are imported, except for a very small proportion of local products. In this respect the urban poverty area is like any other. But in other communities a significant portion of the retail and wholesale trades are owned locally and most of the employees are local. The profits and wages earned by those people are spent locally and serve to help support the local community. A chain of spending and respending is set up which adds strength and variety to the local economy. These internal income flows are of growing importance in contemporary urban areas. Cities used to be noted for their export industries, such as steel in Pittsburgh, automobiles in Detroit, whiskey in Peoria, meat products in Chicago, and so on. Those industries formed the "economic base" around which retail and service industries developed. Although the economic base industries are important, students of urban economics are coming increasingly to recognize that a very large portion of the economy of any metropolitan area is self-sustaining. Each sector of the city's economy strengthens and gives support to the other sectors by means of the income flows that each generates. Cities still specialize in certain types of export products, but they are becoming increasingly general in their economic activities.[4]

The urban poverty area lacks the highly developed internal income flows that might lead to a viable economic pattern. We have already noted that, aside from the irregular economy and relatively small enterprises requiring little capital, business enterprises in the area are not owned by ghetto residents. The incomes earned by the ghetto residents—predominantly from jobs outside the area—are spent in chain supermarkets, furniture and appliance stores, and other enterprises whose ownership and management, and many employees, are almost always of nonghetto origin. The profits and wages received by the outsiders do not come back into the ghetto to

[4]See Wilbur R. Thompson, "Internation and External Factors in the Development of Urban Economies," in Harvey S. Perloff and Lowden Wingo, Jr. (eds.) *Issues in Urban Economics* (Baltimore: Johns Hopkins Press 1965).

support other enterprises or employees. They flow, instead, into the economy of the progressive sector located elsewhere.

These patterns are exaggerated by the low incomes which prevail. Compared with the rest of the economy, relatively small amounts of ghetto incomes are spent on services. With a larger than usual amount spent on goods, the income drain which goods purchases create in any community are proportionately larger for urban poverty areas than for others. Low incomes also mean that housing costs comprise a larger proportion of family budgets than elsewhere. For many ghetto families the cost of housing ranges upward to 35 percent of the family income, thereby transforming a significant portion of ghetto income into withdrawals of capital by owners of rental property.

The income flows help to explain why the welfare system is needed. It stabilizes the ghetto economy. Flows of income in the private sector are generally outward, requiring a compensating inward flow via the public economy. The outward flow of income also helps to explain why increased welfare payments may help the individuals or families who receive them, but have little or no impact on the ghetto economy as a whole. The bulk of the increased payments leaks out rapidly.[5]

Permanent Depression

A condition of permanent depression pervails in urban poverty areas. In other areas the economy may be prosperous, even booming, but in the urban ghettos unemployment will remain high and at levels which would signal a serious depression if they were present in the economy as a whole.

Documentation of the permanent depression of urban poverty areas has only come recently, although the condition has been well known to observers for a long time. In 1968 the Department of Labor reported on a study of employment and unemployment conditions in America's urban slums.[6] Based on the March 1966 *Current Population Survey*, the study showed an overall unemployment rate of about 7.5 percent in the poorest 25 percent of all census tracts in U.S. cities with over 250,000 population (selected on the basis of the 1960 census). The United States as a whole had not seen a national

[5]See Chapter 6 for a detailed discussion of the stabilizing role of welfare payments.
[6]U. S. Department of Labor, "A Sharper Look at Unemployment in U.S. Cities and Slums," (Washington: 1968).

unemployment rate that high since the 1930s. The highest it had been since the end of World War II was 6.8 percent (in 1958, calculated on an annual basis). The national unemployment rate in March 1966 was just half that of the slums: 3.8 percent.

The nonwhite unemployment rate was even higher. Forty-two percent of the residents of these poor census tracts were nonwhite. Their unemployment rate was 9.4 percent—about two and one-half times the national average and approaching the national rates of the more depressed years of the 1930s. Among nonwhite teenagers (14 to 19 years of age) the unemployment rates were 31 percent for boys and 46 percent for girls. It must be pointed out that the sample was quite small, and there is a substantial possibility of error in these last figures.

This preliminary survey was followed up by a more intensive study of urban slum areas in 12 major cities in November 1966. At a time when the national unemployment rate was 3.7 percent, the average unemployment rate in the slums was about 10 percent, or almost three times the national average. Conditions varied from one city slum to another, but all showed serious unemployment problems (see Table 4.1).

The unemployment figures of Table 4.1 include only those who were actively looking for work. They do not include those who should have been in the labor force but were not because they believed, rightly or wrongly, that they could not find a job (or for other reasons). This "nonparticipation rate" in urban poverty areas was 11 percent among men in the 20 to 64 year age group, as compared with a 7 percent rate for men of that age in the economy as a whole.

The unemployment figures also excluded a substantial number of adult men that other statistical sources indicated should be part of the slum area population. The November 1966 survey failed to find between a fifth and a third of the adult men of the slum areas. This parallels the census experience with the undercount problem.[7]

Finally, the unemployment figures did not include persons who were working part time but would have preferred full-time jobs. The November 1966 survey showed that 6.9 percent of all employed persons in urban poverty areas fell into this category. The national figure was 2.3 percent.

[7]One result of the census undercount of men in the slums is a serious political underrepresentation of slum areas. Election districts are based on Census counts of population. The undercount means that the slum consitituency is underrepresented at the local, state and national level.

TABLE 4.1

**Unemployment Rates in United States
Urban Poverty Areas, 1966**

AREA	UNEMPLOYMENT AS A PERCENT OF THE LABOR FORCE
Boston (Roxbury)	6.9
Cleveland (Hough and surrounding neighborhood)	15.6
Detroit (central Woodward area)	10.1
Los Angeles (South Los Angeles)	12.0
New Orleans (several contiguous areas)	10.0
New York (Harlem)	8.1
(East Harlem)	9.0
(Bedford-Stuyvesant)	6.2
Oakland (Bayside)	13.0
Philadelphia (North Philadelphia)	11.0
Phoenix (Salt River Bed area)	13.2
St. Louis (north side)	12.9
San Antonio (east and west sides)	8.1
San Francisco (Mission-Fillmore area)	11.1

SOURCE: U. S. Department of Labor, "A Sharper Look at Unemployment in U. S. Cities and Slums (Washington: 1968).

These latter considerations indicate that the situation in the urban ghetto is worse than the figures on unemployment reveal. In particular, the contrast with the rest of the economy is sharp enough so that national unemployment rates become meaningless in describing conditions in the slums. This does not mean that when unemployment rates decline in the national economy, the slums feel no impact. They do. The manpower resources of urban poverty areas are used by the larger economy, but they form a pool of workers which is always underutilized. Even when markets everywhere else are tight and inflationary pressures in the progressive sectors of the economy are pushing up prices, wages, profits, and interest rates, unemployment in the urban slums rises only to the levels that are characteristic of serious recessions in the economy as a whole. Charles Dickens' famous phrase "It was the best of times, it was the worst of times" applies to this situation with something of an ironic twist: when the first part applies to the rest of the economy, the second part would be a good description of the urban poverty area.

In recent years the federal government's policy of "benign neglect" caused the Department of Labor to abandon its studies of subemployment in the urban ghettos, although it did design an employment survey for the 1970 census that has been partially analyzed by the U. S. Senate Subcommittee on Employment, Manpower and Poverty. The preliminary findings confirm the earlier ones. In 1970 when the national unemployment rate was 4.9 percent, the rate in central city ghetto areas was 9.6 percent. But this includes only those seeking work; adding discouraged workers who would be seeking work if it were available brought the figure to 11 percent. Finally, adjusting the figures for those working part time who would like to work full time raised the proportion of subemployed to 13.3 percent of the labor force.[8] After 1970 national unemployment rates rose to 7 percent and stayed there for several years. If the 1970 relationships continued to hold, the ghetto subemployment rate would have jumped to about 19 percent.

A Model of the Ghetto Economy

We now know enough about the flows of income into and out of the ghetto economy to sketch, in qualitative terms, the chief economic relationships between the ghetto and the outside economy.

Income flows into the ghetto in part as earned income. By far the largest source of earned income is employment in the low-wage industries, which is a fundamental cause, together with high unemployment rates, of the poverty of the ghetto subsystem. A fortunate few have been able to find better employment, but these are the ones who are able to move up and out. Transfer payments supplement earned income, primarily through the welfare system, social security, and medicaid.

These income flows support the three characteristic aspects of

[8]William Spring, Bennett Harrison, and Thomas Vietorisz, "Crisis of the Underemployed," *New York Times Magazine*, Nov. 5, 1972, p. 42ff.

the ghetto economy that most clearly distinguish it from the rest of the economy—the private business sector, with its special "penny capitalism" aspects that derive from the low-income nature of its customers; the irregular economy; and the criminal sector, with its numbers gambling, loan sharking, narcotics, prostitution, and theft, all interrelated and all an integral part of the whole. These three aspects of the ghetto economy are themselves intertwined and overlapping.

The outward flows of income, capital, and human resources to the rest of the economy serve to keep the ghetto in a permanently underdeveloped state and feed the economic interests outside the ghetto that have developed around those income flows. Some are relatively narrow and special: the slum lord, the criminal overlord, the owner of ghetto business enterprises. Others are broader. The entire economy outside of the ghetto benefits from the income, capital, and manpower resources that are drawn out, just as it benefits from a pool of low-wage labor that provides relatively low-cost services to those outside.

These economic relationships are sketched in Figure 4.1. They help to explain why the ghetto seems to be a necessary and permanent feature of the economic and social order, why it is partially cut off from the economic forces that operate in the rest of the economy, and why efforts to ameliorate ghetto poverty seem to peter out into ineffectualness.

A study by Richard L. Schaffer of the Bedford-Stuyvesant ghetto in New York, now the nation's largest, confirms the importance of the

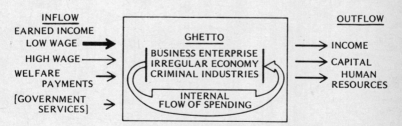

The level of income in the ghetto economy depends upon maintaining the inflow of income. Welfare payments play a crucial role, enabling society to maintain the ghetto at any level of relative poverty desired, thereby offsetting the outflows of resources and stabilizing both the ghetto subsystem *and* its place in the economy as a whole.

FIGURE 4.1   A Model of the Ghetto Economy.

drain of income from the inner city gettos.[9] In 1969 the area had a population of 220,000 and a total inflow of income of about $853 million. Shaffer was able to identify and estimate outflows of income totaling $640 million. The outflows included such items as:

Housing disinvestment—$25 million
Net profits from business and housing—20 million
Narcotics—30 million

The total of $75 million was about one-fourth of the area's $276 million of earnings from wages and other income. By comparison, total savings of area residents amounted to only about $20 million.

Shaffer was also able to document the great importance of government as a source of income for the ghetto. Government services provided to the Bedford-Stuyvesant area in 1969 cost about $167 million and transfer payments added another $122 million, for a total income from government sources of almost $289 million. This sum was larger than the earned income of the area. The total of all taxes collected was only $85 million, or less than one-third of the government contribution. By contrast, nearby Borough Park, a slightly larger middle-income area, paid $198 million in taxes and received just $191 million in government services and transfers. The ghetto could not sustain itself without the inflow of payments from government.[10]

Circular Causation and Cumulative Effects

The condition of the ghetto economy is a classic example of circular causation in social processes.[11] The ghetto economy perpetuates its own poverty. Low incomes mean low levels of living. This style of life has obvious deficiencies: poor food, bad housing, poor health, and bad sanitation. These conditions lead back to low labor

[9]Richard L. Schaffer, "Income Flows in Urban Poverty Ereas: A Comparison of the Community Income Accounts of Bedford-Stuyvesant and Borough Park" (Unpublished doctoral dissertation, New York University, 1972).

[10]See Robert S. Browne, "Cash Flows in a Ghetto Community", Review of Black Political Economy, Vol. 1, No. 3 (Winter- Spring 1971), pp. 28-39, for further analysis of the outward flow of resources from the ghetto.

[11]See Gunnar Myrdal, Asian Drama (New York: Random House, 1968), Vol. III, Appendix 2. The more important sections of this appendix are 2, 4, 5, 8-11. Further references to the theory of circular causation and "vicious circles" are in footnotes on pp. 1844-1845.

productivity and a perpetuation of low incomes.[12] The drain of resources out of urban poverty areas—manpower, capital, income—serves to reinforce the poverty. Social overhead capital is inadequate. The public services which might overcome part of the deficiencies in private incomes are insufficient. In particular, deficiencies in the educational system lead to inadequate training, low skill levels, and low productivity.

Employment patterns, especially in low-wage industries and the irregular economy, reinforce the pattern of poverty and create barriers to movement of workers into the high-wage sectors outside the urban poverty area. At the same time those ghetto residents who do move up and out take with them much of the entrepreneurship that development of the ghetto economy requires.

Economic development is further retarded by ineffective instruments for local control: the destinies of urban poverty areas have been largely in the hands of outsiders. Weak political representation and control of local governments by an "establishment" power structure have kept the poor out of power. The result is a weak infrastructure of voluntary organizations and a low level of popular participation in the decision-making process. This, in turn, retards the development of decision-making and entrepreneurial abilities. The dual lack of entrepreneurship and effective power means that decisions which affect the ghetto economy will be made largely by the outsiders who dominate the decision-making process.

One result has been that many policies and programs have hurt the ghetto rather than helped as intended. Welfare payments have tended to weaken attachment to the labor market. Urban renewal has increased the overcrowding of housing rather than diminished it. Highway construction has had the same effect. Educational programs have been unable to prevent a serious deterioration of the schools. Even the benefits of low-cost housing have been relatively small compared with the incomes generated for nonghetto residents.

In this context the racial attitudes of whites and the long heritage of black repression takes on its key significance. Together they have kept the great majority of blacks in the ghetto, unable to move out of the vicious circle of self-generating poverty which prevails there.

The pattern of the ghetto economy, then, presents a series of self-reinforcing influences:

[12]Pedro Belli, "The Economic Implications of Malnutrition: The Dismal Science Revisited," *Economic Development and Cultural Change*, Vol. 20, No. 1 (October 1971), pp. 1-23, provides a detailed review of empirical studies on the relationship between malnutrition, health, and intelligence that shows the process of circular causation at work. See also Irving Leveson, Boris Ullman, and Gregory Wassall, "Effects of Health on Education and Productivity," *Inquiry*, Vol. VI, No. 4 (December 1969), pp. 3-11.

1. Poverty breeds a style of life which reinforces the conditions which lead to poverty.

2. Resources which might lead to betterment and development are drained out.

3. Lack of political power has brought public programs which are often harmful to the ghetto economy.

4. White attitudes toward race have kept most of the ghetto residents from moving out.

A social system in which a pattern of circular causation functions will generally reach an equilibrium in which causative factors balance each other. It may be a moving equilibrium if growth processes operate. If outside forces impinge on the equilibrium and if they set up secondary effects moving in the same direction, a self-sustaining process of growth can be established, particularly if the social system can move beyond the position, or threshold, from which the old equilibrium can no longer be reestablished. These basic propositions from the theory of growth and economic development embody the concept of cumulative effects: circular causation can lead to maintenance of the existing equilibrium, but it can also lead to cumulative movements toward either growth or retrogression.

Economic growth is particularly difficult for the ghetto economy. Its weak infrastructure, the lack of local initiative and entrepreneurship, and the shortage of capital make it difficult to generate a growth process. These factors are an integral part of the self-generating poverty cycle. More important, the tendency for resources and income to drain out of the ghetto economy means that even if the forces of development were to appear, much of their strength would be dissipated before they had a significant impact on the ghetto itself. Any program or programs that seek to improve the economy of urban poverty areas must reverse the drain of skilled manpower, capital, and income if a cumulative process of growth is to be established.

Rather than growth, a cumulative process of retrogression has been the fate of urban poverty areas over the last twenty years. The key outside influence was the migration of the 1950s and the ensuing population explosion. These demographic changes both expanded the size of the problem and worsened the condition of a social and economic system already suffering from permanent depression and a self-reinforcing pattern of underdevelopment. Retrogressive forces were set in motion which worsened the poverty, speeded up the drain of resources, and further weakened the social and economic infrastructure. Only massive increases in public expenditure programs have been able to stem the tide and recreate (perhaps) a new equilibrium.

Conditions may be getting worse rather than better. In the early 1960s black incomes seemed to be falling further behind those of whites. In more recent years the data on black family incomes shows a narrowing gap between blacks and whites. Most or all of this improvement disappears, however, when allowance is made for the fact that husband and wife both work in a larger proportion of black families than white and for the tendency of these studies to seriously underreport data on blacks in central city poverty neighborhoods. In addition, there is some evidence that whatever gains blacks as a whole are making relative to whites are concentrated outside the ghettos. Meanwhile, the gap in wages between low-and high-wage employment has tended to widen, and housing segregation has tended to grow in spite of a movement of blacks into suburban areas. At the same time a major crisis in youth employment in the central cities has appeared, accompanied by a large upsurge in crime and drug use. As the second wave of the urban ghetto population explosion starts (the children who comprised the first wave in the early 1950s are now entering young adulthood), a second lost generation is about to appear in the cities. The current picture is one of continuation of ghetto conditions and the circular causation of poverty and deprivation.[13]

[13]Alan Batchelder, "The Decline in the Relative Income of Negro Men," *Quarterly Journal of Economics*, Vol. 78, No. 4 (November 1964), pp. 525-548. "Recent Trends in Social and Economic Conditions of Negroes in the United States", *Current Population Reports*, Series p-23, No. 26 (Washington: U. S. Department of Commerce, Bureau of the Census, July 1968), presents data showing relative improvement in black incomes, but serious questions can be raised about the quality of this data. For a critique and defense of this report, see "Employment and Manpower Problems in the Cities," *Hearings*, Joint Economic Committee, May 28-June 6, 1968 (Washington: U. S. Government Printing Office, 1968), pp. 97-107. Daniel P. Moynihan, "Memorandum for the President," *New York Times*, March 1, 1970, suggested "benign neglect" of the racial problem on the basis of data showing black improvement relative to white. The data Moynihan used were criticized by Andrew F. Brimmer, "Economic Progress of Negroes in the United States: The Deepening Schism," Address at Tuskegee Institute, March 22, 1970 (mimeo), reported in the *New York Times* of the same date. Brimmer also argued that there was a growing income gap among blacks with the poor black family making no progress and perhaps falling further behind. Barry Bluestone, "The Secular Deterioration of Wage Terms Among Industries in the United States" (Ann Arbor: University of Michigan, mimeo, 1968) presents evidence that the wage gap between low-and high-wage employment has tended to widen in recent years. Reynolds Farley and Karl E. Taeuber, "Population Trends and Residential Segregation Since 1960," *Science*, Vol. 159, No. 3818 (March 1, 1968), pp. 953-956, documents the increase in housing segregation. The

The Urban Ghetto as a Residual Subsystem

The urban ghetto is a world apart. It serves an essential need of our society as a repository for those residual people for whom the social and economic system has little or no use.

Every social system rejects individuals who do not meet the standards established for membership in the various subsystems which make up the larger social order. Rejection mechanisms are many and varied. For example, the requirements for acceptance into the northeastern suburbs of Detroit—one of the subsystems that make up the whole—include the income required to buy or rent an expensive home. Test scores and grades are important for admission to college. Certain requirements must be met to obtain a civil service job. Formal or informal restrictions keep some country clubs and fraternal organizations free of Jews or blacks. A middle-class pattern of behavior is necessary for acceptance in the typical suburban community. Examples can be multiplied, but the principle is clear: each of the subsystems into which the social system divides itself accepts or rejects individuals according to its own formal or informal criteria. One of the most unfortunate aspects of our society is that race is one of the major criteria for acceptance or rejection.

Rejection from one subsystem of the "desirable" sectors of society does not mean rejection from all, in most cases. The individual or family unable to find a place in one will usually find another. There may be frustrations and disappointments, but a place is usually found. Most people are not rejected out of the social system as a whole.

But some are. Dangerous or particularly bizarre (irrational) behavior takes some to mental hospitals. Crimes draw others to prisons. Others gravitate to the urban ghetto, often because of a syndrome of ghetto characteristics such as race, poor education, low skill, and lack of adaptability to the behavior pattern of the more successful sectors of social order. Mental hospitals, jails, and slums—these are the chief depositories our society has created for those who cannot fit in or be fitted into the dominant way of life. They make up the residual subsystems into which society's rejects congregate.

An example will show how the mechanism works. The black

current crisis in youth employment is examined in The Twentieth Century Fund, *The Job Crisis for Black Youth* (New York: Praeger, 1971). Recent data on the relative economic position of blacks and whites is in "The Social and Economic Status of Negroes in the United States, 1970" *Current Population Reports,* Series p-23, No. 38 (Washington: U. S. Department of Commerce, Bureau of the Census, July 1971).

sharecropper, poor, almost uneducated, lacking in skills, who found employment in agriculture in the Mississippi delta region in 1950 found that he was redundant there in 1955. He was rejected from the economic system in which he had formerly been able to subsist, even though he was at the bottom of the economic and social order. Cast out there, he made his way to the ghetto of a southern city or a northern city. He moved to the place where other economic rejects also had moved. Partly by choice, and partly because there was no other place to go, he ended up in the urban ghetto. Examination of the characteristics of ghetto residents tell us the chief factors which cause rejection from the progressive sector of the economy.

Race: blacks, Puerto Ricans, Mexican Americans and other minority groups.

Recent arrival: migrants from the rural South, Southwest, and Puerto Rico.

Cultural differences: persons with a cultural background different from the white middle-class culture.

Low productivity: low earning power resulting from lack of skills, poor education, bad health, old age, and related factors.

Low income: inability to live in the style of the white middle class because of inadequate financial resources.

People rejected from the social-economic system are not scattered at random. They do not stay in the suburbs, or in southern agriculture, or in the universities, if they are caught up in the rejection mechanisms. The residuals tend to collect or be collected at specific points in the system as a whole.

Residual subsystems are usually separated from the functioning central sectors of the social order by barriers of various types. Mental hospitals and jails are walled or fenced, and entry is by a formal process of legal commitment. The urban ghetto is different. There are no physical barriers between the ghetto and the rest of society, and no formal methods by which individuals are "committed" to life in the ghetto. The barriers are economic and social rather than physical, and the selection process is informal.

The barriers between the urban ghetto and the rest of the economic and social system do not cut off the ghetto completely. A substantial number of individuals do move out and up into other sectors of society. Others move down and into the ghetto. Individuals are always moving from one subsystem to another in our highly mobile society. The process is not that simple, however, and in the urban ghetto there exist three barriers that are insurmountible for most residents.

1. Mobility outward for many people is not based on merit, or even income, which often acts as a proxy for merit. Race is an important criterion for movement out. It is a barrier for blacks and Puerto Ricans that is not present for whites.

2. The culture of the ghetto creates and fosters a way of life that makes it difficult for individuals to be accepted in other sectors of the economy and society. This includes such factors as work habits and attitudes toward work developed in the irregular economy and patterns of behavior fostered by the welfare economy.

3. The fact that the urban ghetto is a depository for people rejected from society influences the attitudes of the rest of society toward the ghetto. These attitudes are reflected in inadequate provision of public services, such as education and health, which tend to preserve ghettorization and reduce the upward mobility of ghetto residents.

The informal and unseen barriers show up in the economic statistics of inordinately high levels of unemployment, relatively low income levels, relatively low residential mobility, and many other distinctive features of the ghetto. More important, they tend to keep within the ghetto a large number of people whose native abilities and potential for development are largely wasted. This waste of human resources is particularly tragic in the case of young people whose chances for the good life are greatly diminished because of the ghetto environment in which they are born.

When the process of rejection from the larger economy takes place on a larger scale and at a faster pace than the movement up and out of the ghetto, the urban ghettos expand and grow, and conditions there deteriorate. This is exactly what happened in the 1950s and 1960s. The two movements are perhaps balanced at the present time—and there are some indications that in several large cities the ghettos may be shrinking—but there is no reason to believe that either continued growth or gradual shrinkage of the ghettos is an inevitable trend.

The process itself is diagrammed in simple fashion in Figure 4.2.

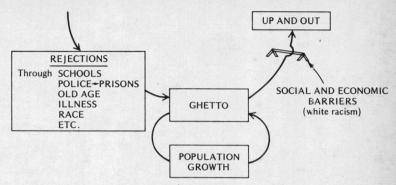

The sophisticated reader will recognize an ironic similarity between this schema and Marx's description of the "reserve army of the unemployed" in Volume I of *Capital*. The difference is that Marx felt his reserve army would inevitably grow, while in this analysis the growth of the ghetto depends on the relative size of three flows: population growth plus rejections *versus* the movement up and out.

FIGURE 4.2   The Ghetto as a Residual Subsystem

Policy Strategy for Workable Solutions

The national economy is not a seamless web of relationships that make up a unified articulated whole. Rather, the urban ghetto emerges as a quasi-enclave. It is part of the national economy and is affected by what goes on in the national economy. But the connecting links are seriously deficient. Barriers exist which prevent, for example, an increase in gross national product from having the same effects on the ghetto that it has in the rest of the economy. Barriers prevent the rising living standards due to economic growth from having the same effects in the urban ghetto that they have elsewhere.

The quasi enclave of the ghetto has developed its own characteristic system of relationships within which its inhabitants function. We have described some of the economic aspects of this social subsystem: the low-wage sector, the irregular economy and the welfare economy. We have noted some of the results: poverty, permanent depression, and underdevelopment. We have also identified some of the relationships between the ghetto subsystem and the larger social system: the flow of transfer payments into the ghetto which serves to stabilize and helps to support it and the outward flow of capital, income, and human skills. And we have emphasized the fact that the ghetto subsystem tends to preserve the conditions which lead to ghettoization, generates the attitudes which keep people ghettoized, and largely prevents a process of economic development from getting started. The ghetto subsystem, in short, tends to preserve itself in a relatively static position, and reproduce itself from generation to generation. It may even grow in size, as it has done in the last fifteen years.

This concept of the urban ghetto as a residual subsystem—a place where society maintains its outcasts and semioutcasts—is essential to the development of policy and programs for the ghetto. In this context the welfare system or other forms of income maintenance are not solutions, but ameliorative devices. Improved education and training programs may help individuals, but they will not transform the ghetto unless they operate on a scale large enough to enable more people to overcome the barriers to outward and upward mobility than are moving inward and downward to the ghetto. Better housing may improve living conditions, but it will not necessarily make an impact on ghettoization. Our experience with public low cost housing confirms that view. Better health services and other public facilities, while also needed and desirable in themselves, likewise fail to attack the basic causes of ghettoization.

This is not to say that concerted and large-scale programs to improve incomes, education and training, housing, and health, and to provide jobs, are doomed to failure. If they are large enough and if they are sustained long enough, they can make an important contribution to a solution of the problem. But they are addressed to symptoms rather than basic causes.

The fundamental causes of urban ghettos are the rejection mechanisms of our society. The ghettos will be with us until those social processes are changed: (1) The rejection mechansims must be identified and their operation modified or ended. In particular, the relationship of blacks to the larger opportunity system must be drastically transformed. In the long run this will mean fundamental social and political changes as well as economic. (2) Better feedback mechanisms must be developed to bring society's rejects back into the mainstream. The greatest potential lies in employment and job training, but they have never been used on the massive scale required.

It is in connection with programs to transform the rejection mechanisms and generate better feedbacks that programs for income maintenance, education, housing, health, and all the rest begin to make sense. Standing by themselves, or even used together, they can have little effect because they do not change the fundamental workings of a social system that continually creates residuals. But they can be useful when developed in conjunction with policies and programs directed toward significant changes in some of the more dysfunctional aspects of our economic and social system.

CHAPTER 5

Discrimination and Coerced Labor

The conventional wisdom among economists emphasizes two different approaches to racial discrimination and economic disparities between blacks and whites. One is an extension of utility theory and is closely associated with Gary Becker, whose book *The Economics of Discrimination*[1] has become a classic of economic analysis. The second approach has been developed out of work on human capital and stresses education, training, health, and other personal characteristics of low-income groups that are associated with poverty. The best and most recent statement of this approach is Lester C. Thurow, *Poverty and Discrimination*.[2] Both of these approaches to the problem of racial discrimination have the comforting quality of drawing attention away from the institutionalized sources of the problem analyzed in this book. Both suggest that people, rather than social and economic structures, have to be changed—Becker, that whites must be changed in order to reduce the "taste for discrimination," and the human capitalists, that blacks should be changed to eliminate the poor education and low productivity that are associated with low incomes.

Neither the utility nor human capital theories take into account the earlier and classic hypothesis that low incomes for minority groups, including women, results from crowding them into a relatively small number of menial occupations while excluding them from higher paying jobs. The "crowding" phenomenon then creates a variant of coerced labor, other forms of which are slavery, serfdom, and the sharecropping-debt tenure system.[3] Among other things, this analy-

[1]Gary S. Becker, *The Economics of Discrimination*, 2nd ed. (Chicago: University of Chicago Press, 1957).

[2]Lester C. Thurow, *Poverty and Discrimination* (Washington: Brookings Institution, 1969).

[3]The classic paper on the crowding hypothesis is Francis Y. Edgeworth, "Equal Pay to Men and Women for Equal Work," *Economic Journal*, Vol. XXXII (December 1922), pp. 431-457. Edgeworth's analysis built on the work of Millicent Fawcett, including "The Position of Women in Economic Life," in W. H. Dawson (ed.), *After-War Problems* (London: Allen and Unwin, 1917), pp. 191-215, and "Equal Pay for Equal Work," *Economic Journal*, Vol. XXVIII (March 1918), pp. 1-6.

Taussig's concept of noncompeting groups is somewhat similar. See Frank Taussig, *Principles of Economics* (New York: Macmillan, 1946), Vol. II, pp. 234-245, and N. D. Glenn, "Occupational Benefits to Whites from the Subordination of Negroes," *American Sociological Review*, Vol. 28 (June 1963), pp. 443-448. Barbara Bergmann's development of the crowding hypothesis is in "Effect on White Incomes of Discrimination in Employment," *Journal of Political Economy*, Vol. 29, No. 2 (Mar.-Apr. 1971), pp. 294-313. On the concept of coerced labor, see Robert Evans, "Some Notes on Coerced Labor," *Journal of Economic History*, Vol. XXX, No. 4 (Dec. 1970), pp. 861-866, and the references noted therein.

sis indicts the structure of social and economic institutions as one source of the crowding of occupations that brings poverty.

The issues involved in these theories of discrimination are important. Becker's utility theory is an appropriate place to start.

Becker on Discrimination

Becker's theory of discrimination fills a gap in the theory of the competitive market. In that theory the interplay of individual consumers desiring to maximize their utility with producers seeking to maximize their gains brings a social optimum in which net benefits are maximized. Any departure of actual behavior from the assumptions about consumers or producers results in a less than optimum solution in which the social product is reduced and some producers or consumers, or both, receive less than they would if the purely competitive market solution were achieved. Racial discrimination is excluded from this model by the assumptions made about individual behavior and by the driving forces of competition, which press economic units to maximize their net gains.[4] In this analysis there is no place for such irrational behavior as racial prejudice.

Becker's contribution was to make a place for it. He postulated that participants in a transaction may have a "taste for discrimination" which influences their behavior along with the expected gains from the transaction. A white employer with a taste for discrimination against blacks will be willing to give up a certain amount of profit in order to hire white workers instead of blacks. A white employee with a taste for discrimination will be willing to take a somewhat lower wage in order to avoid working alongside blacks. The strength of the taste for discrimination can be measured by the amount of income each would be willing to forego in order to indulge his taste for discrimination.

This is the key to Becker's analysis: As a market imperfection, the taste for discrimination causes a reduced money income for the one who practices discrimination as well as for the person who is discriminated against. This conclusion is inherent in the theoretical base since it is assumed (advocates would say proven) that the competitive market results in maximum net gains for society. If that is true, any imperfection must be accompanied by losses that are

---

[4]W. H. Hutt, *The Economics of the Colour Bar* (London: Institute of Economic Affairs, 1964), forcefully presents the argument that the competitive economy is color blind.

somehow shared to a greater or lesser degree by the participants in the market transactions.[5]

Becker goes on to derive a series of theorems relating to discrimination. Discrimination will harm those discriminated against more than those who do the discriminating if the former are an economic minority supplying only a relatively small protion of the labor supply. The wages of workers who are the object of discrimination will be reduced while those workers who are not discriminated against will earn higher wages. However, employers will lose because they will have to pay more for the labor that they hire. And, if the minority workers attempt to retaliate against discrimination, they will lose more than will those who do the discriminating.

Becker's elegant analysis leaves one with the uneasy feeling that it rescues utility theory from a tight corner without throwing much light on the world of black-white economic relationships. It focuses on white attitudes rather than the functional economic relationships described in this book, and it leads to the implicit policy conclusion that if white attitudes were changed, all would be well. Policy should be directed against white racial feelings through the educational system; as they are gradually changed, the economic situation of blacks will slowly improve. There is little else that one can do. Becker, to his credit, does not make this argument, but it is inherent in his assumptions.

The Human Capital Approach

The second approach, that of the human capital theorists, has its roots in the classic study of the American racial problem by Gunnar Myrdal.[6] Myrdal analyzed the self-reinforcing conditions of poverty and deprivation which keep blacks in a disadvantaged position. Blacks have high unemployment rates and low wages, are concentrated in menial occupations, obtain inferior educations, and have inadequate health care. All of these disadvantages reinforce each other and lead to perpetuation of black disadvantages in a vicious circle of poverty and lack of opportunity. In this view the heritage of

[5]Extension of Becker's theory has shown that net gains can be made by whites from discrimination against blacks, and that Becker is wrong in arguing that both the discriminator and discriminatee necessarily are worse off. See Thurow, *op. cit.*, pp. 112-116, and Anne O. Krueger, "The Economics of Discrimination," *Journal of Political Economy*, Vol LXXI, No. 5 (October 1963), pp. 481-486.

[6]Gunnar Myrdal, *An American Dilemma* (New York: Harper & Row, 1944). Myrdal's book open the path for development of the human capital approach to the problem, but, needless to say, his analysis was far more complex and sophisticated.

slavery is of major importance, for it imposed on blacks the original disadvantages from which they have been unable to recover.

The human capital theorists build upon this analysis to advocate a variety of government-sponsored programs to eradicate the problem. Better education, manpower training and employment programs, and improved health care for blacks—programs designed to increase productivity—will enable blacks to raise their incomes and break out of the self-reinforcing conditions of poverty. Most advocates of this position recognize that discrimination in the labor market will have to be eliminated if ameliorative programs are to have the expected breakthrough effect, but major stress is placed on the need for human capital investment in education, training, and health care.

Thurow takes a variant of this position. He seeks to reconcile it with the fact that a much larger proportion of blacks than whites are poor and the fact that black poverty seems to be less readily ended. He argues that discrimination is indeed a factor: whites seek to maximize their utility, as in Becker's analysis, but with social distance from blacks as one element in their choices among alternatives. There are a number of varieties of discrimination, he argues, in employment, wages, occupational choice, investment in human capital, and so on. Some conflict with the others, but all have one characteristic in common: whites are in a monopolistic position relative to blacks and use their economic advantage to increase their gains at the expense of blacks and to maintain social distance. In the end, however, Thurow advocates investment in human capital as the key to breaking the barriers of discrimination: "Attacking human capital discrimination will not raise Negro incomes by itself, since wage, employment, and occupational discrimination also have to be eliminated, but eliminating human capital discrimination would make the enforcement of these other types difficult in the absence of government discrimination."[7]

Thurow's position is typical of the programmatic, reforming liberal: enough investment in human capital will do the job if supplemented by elimination of government support for other forms of discrimination and perhaps active government efforts to prevent them.

The Crowding Hypothesis

Neither the utility nor the human capital approaches to the problem of minority group disadvantages give adequate attention to

[7]Thurow, *op, cit.*, p. 138.

the crowding of minorities into low-wage occupations. Analysis of that phenomenon was first developed in modern economics during the drive for women's rights in the period from 1890 to 1925 and culminated in Francis Y. Edgeworth's classic 1922 article on equal pay for men and women.[8] It is by far the broadest of the theories of discrimination since it can be applied to minorities with any characteristics and involves both individual tastes *and* structural elements in the economy. In so doing it suggests that changes must occur in both people and in economic institutions.

The crowding hypothesis is based on the observed phenomenon that minority groups are crowded into a relatively small number of menial occupations. The crowding depresses wage rates in these occupations because of the artificially increased supply of labor there. Meanwhile, the supply of labor in other occupations is decreased, leading to wage rates somewhat higher than they would otherwise be in those occupations. These initial effects have a variety of other implications, which we shall examine presently.

To illustrate the hypothesis, we start with two occupations, A and B, which require the same level of skills, and examine, first, the results in a color-blind economy and, second, the results in an economy with racial discrimination.

In the color-blind economy, assuming competition in the labor market, the forces of supply and demand result in the same wage rate in the two occupations. Any wage differential will cause labor to shift from one to the other, since skill levels are the same, until wages are equalized. Furthermore, employers will hire workers in each occupation up to the point at which the amount added to total revenue by the additional worker is just equal to the wage paid (the theory of marginal productivity applies here). The results are shown in Figure 5.1.

Now we close one occupation to blacks and force them into jobs in the other occupation, reserving the closed occupation to whites. Wage rates in the two occupations will differ, and the numbers employed will also shift. We look first at the decline of wages in the occupation into which the minority group is crowded, in Figure 5.2 on page 66.

Meanwhile, wages rise in the occupation from which minorities are excluded, as shown in Figure 5-3 on page 67.

We can note a number of corollary propositions suggested by the simple analysis of the wage and employment effects of crowding. First, there is no reason to believe that total employment need be

[8]Edgeworth, *op, cit.*

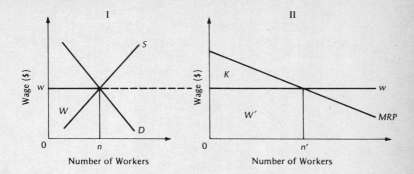

FIGURE 5.1 Color Blind Economy. Two Occupations with Similar Skill Levels. Wages in both occupations are the same, since skills are interchangeable. In Diagram I the wage in both occupations is determined by the interaction of demand and supply at level *w*, while *n* workers are employed. *W* is the total wage bill. Diagram II shows the individual employer hiring *n'* workers at wage *w*, given the marginal revenue product[9] as shown by *MRP*. *W'* is the total wage bill of the individual employer, and *K* is the amount retained for payments to other factors of production, such as capital.

reduced. Wages will fall in the crowded occupation (A) until all those who are willing to work at those wages are employed. Similarly, the higher wage in the other occupation (B) will clear the market and assure employment of all willing workers. These conclusions assume, however, that the level of aggregate demand is sustained at full-employment levels to assure jobs for the entire work force.

A more important corollary is the effect on work incentives among the minority group. Since wages in the crowded occupation will be abnormally low, the incentive to work (as against leisure time or irregular occupations) will be reduced. As a result, labor force participation rates among the minority group will be lower than among the majority, whose higher wages encourage a greater amount of work as compared to leisure. This expected result is consistent with the empirical finding that labor force participation rates are higher among whites than among blacks, although other factors are undoubtedly at work as well.

[9]Marginal revenue product is the name given by economists to the additional revenues obtained by adding one unit of a factor of production to a fixed amount of other factors, for example, adding an additional worker to the existing work force in a manufacturing plant.

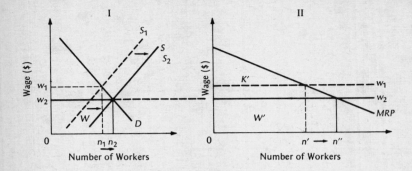

FIGURE 5.2   "Crowding" Reduces Wages Rates in Occupation A. In Diagram I the increase in supply of labor in occupation A, due to "crowding," shifts the supply curve from S_1 to S_2, with demand conditions remaining unchanged. The wage falls from w_1 to w_2 and the number employed increases from n_1 to n_2. The total amount of wage paid (W) may or may not increase. In Diagram II the individual employer increases the number of workers he hires from n' to n'' (his wage bill, W', may or may not increase). However, the value of the marginal product has fallen, since w_2 is less than w_1. As we shall see, this indicates a misallocation of resources from society's point of view. In addition, the amount paid to other factors (K') rises.

Related to this phenomenon is the movement of minority groups into criminal occupations. Low wages in menial occupations, together with exclusion from higher wage occupations, provides strong incentives to try for the large rewards available from crime. This channeling of minorities into crime by economic forces has been characteristic of our history, attracting immigrant minorities from the Irish to Jews to Italians and now to blacks and Puerto-Ricans. The majority of any minority group will undoubtedly be honest and law-abiding citizens, but there are strong economic incentives that draw a larger proportion of minority groups into criminal activities.

Another result of crowding is payment of substandard wages to minority employees when they are able to get jobs in the higher wage occupations. For a black engineer, the alternative employment is at a low wage in a menial occupation. He is willing, therefore, to accept less than the standard wage for engineers. Employers are aware of

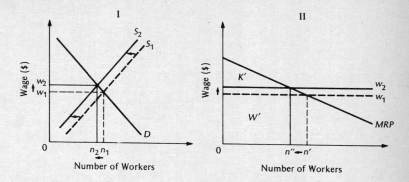

FIGURE 5.3 "Crowding" of the Minority in Occupation A Causes Wages to Rise in Occupation B. In Diagram I the decreased supply of workers in occupation B due to exclusion of blacks shifts the supply curve to the left of S_1 to S_2. With no change in demand the wage rate increases from w_1 to w_2 and employment falls from n_1 to n_2. These changes are reflected in Diagram II in individual employers' reordering of their activities. They hire fewer workers because of the higher wage rate (n' falls to n''). Labor productivity at the margin is higher than it was before (w_2 is greater than w_1). While the total wage bill (W') may or may not change, the amount paid to other factors of production (K') is reduced.

this situation, and enough of them take advantage of it to create the pattern of unequal wage rates for the same job between whites and blacks, men and women, and other groups subjected to crowding. In recent years there has been some modification of this unequal pay syndrome because of federal government pressure on firms producing under government contract, but differential pay is still widely prevalent.[10]

Crowding of minority groups into menial occupations brings about a noticeable misallocation of resources. Employment in the low-wage occupations is greater than it would be without crowding, while there is less employment in other occupations. This can be seen by

[10]Stefan Michaelson, "Incomes of Racial Minorities" (Washington: Brookings Institution, 1968, mimeo) has shown that the greatest reduction in black-white income differentials can be achieved by equalizing pay within occupations. Correcting the maldistribution of blacks among occupations, while leaving intact the wage differentials within occupations, would have a much smaller effect.

referring back to Figures 5.2 and 5.3. Lower wages in the crowded occupations result in more employment there. Higher wages in other occupations are accompanied by reduced employment in those jobs. At the same time a larger total return to other factors of production (K' in Figure 5.2) encourages expanded employment in the crowded occupations, while a smaller return in the other occupations (K' in Figure 5.3) reduces employment there. The result is misallocation of all kinds of resources into the low-wage occupations and industries. Both labor and capital could be shifted to uses in which returns are higher. This is a loss which must be borne by everyone. Although it is not obvious at first glance that overexpansion of low-wage industries and overemployment in low-wage occupations is harmful to the economy as a whole, that is, in fact, the case. Shifting a worker from an occupation in which he produces goods worth $1.50 per hour to one in which he produces $3.50 per hour brings a net benefit of $2.00 per hour to the economy as a whole.

As for the employer, crowding does not bring him any special benefits or losses if competition prevails. Even though he pays low wages to some workers, competition will push his profits down to the normal level. Only if the employer is in a monopolistic position can he gain from crowding, and then only if he hires enough low-wage workers to more than offset the higher amounts he pays in other occupations.

The chief gainers from crowding are workers from the majority population. They earn more than they would if greater competition for jobs from minority groups were present. This has always been true and helps to explain why workers seek to maintain segregated occupational patterns.

Crowding and Coerced Labor

Coerced labor is a phenomenon found widely through history. Slavery is its most obvious form. Labor is coerced by the law which declares slaves to be property, enabling owners to exploit them much as horses and cows are used to produce for man. Serfdom, in its many forms of dependent peasantry, is another ancient form of coerced labor. The military draft is a contemporary form. The essential element in all types of coerced labor is exploitation of the worker: he receives less than he otherwise would if he were free to do something else.

Two conditions are necessary for coerced labor. First, there must be a shortage of workers for the jobs to be done. In a free labor market the shortage would normally lead to higher pay for the worker, to the disadvantage of his employer. Coercion is used in order to enable the employer (slaveholder, seigneur, government) to obtain the labor at reduced cost and retain a larger portion of the gains than he would otherwise get.

Second, alternative opportunities for the worker must be absent or substantially reduced. If the serf or slave or draftee can evade the system, he cannot be coerced into accepting substandard pay. Thus, most systems of coerced labor use the power of the state, through its armies, police, and penal system, to limit the opportunities open to coerced labor and force it to remain in its exploited condition.

But not always. The sharecropping and debt tenure system in the South after the Civil War (which remained strong through the 1940s and some remnants are still found) was enforced by economic forces, legal constraints, and community pressures that were often more informal than formal. This is not the place for a history and analysis of the sharecropping-debt tenure system in the South, even though a thorough treatment of the system has never been written, but the chief elements are important, because many blacks in this country came from that background. A sharecropper used the land owned by someone else, with the landlord often supplying seed and tools and sometimes living expenses. In return, the landlord received a share of the receipts after he was repaid the cost of seed and sustenance. Usually the landlord received half and the tenant half. This system grew up after the Civil War when former slaveowners had land but no labor, while the former slaves had labor but no land. It was open to much abuse. The black farmer had little education, and the white landowner usually sold the crop and kept the books.

Simple sharecropping gave way to a system of debt tenure. After a bad crop year the tenant might not have earned enough to carry him through the year to the next harvest and to provide seed for the next crop. Money for those purposes would have to be borrowed, either from the landlord or a storekeeper in town. Debt could then become a legal way of tying the tenant to the land. Debts had to be settled before a family was allowed to leave the land, and the debts had a habit of persisting from year to year. This happened throughout the rural South with poor whites as well as poor blacks—in much the same way as the Biblical Joseph was able to enslave the Egyptian peasantry for the Pharaohs by using the stored surplus of seven fat years to make loans during the ensuing seven lean years.

Although sharecropping and debt tenure were used to tie labor to the land, lack of opportunity elsewhere was one of the chief reasons for the long retention of coerced labor in the South. Industry was slow in developing, poverty prevented acquisition of western land, and northern industry was surfeited with hordes of unskilled laborers immigrating from Europe. Only with the ending of immigration and the start of World War I did economic opportunity open the way to ending the coerced labor of the rural South. From then on the black population of the South was able to migrate north to opportunity— and the urban ghetto.

There a different form of coerced labor appeared. By excluding blacks from higher paying occupations and crowding them into menial jobs the pattern of exploitation was continued, but in a different (and less intense?) form. The pattern was first established in southern cities during the 1890s, when the great depression of that decade, particularly strong in agriculture, forced significant numbers of blacks off the farms in spite of sharecropping and debt tenure. Moving into southern cities, they were met with an upsurge of Jim Crow legislation that imposed rigid segregation and largely eliminated their right to vote.[11] Concurrently, blacks were driven out of a number of occupations they had hitherto filled, such as the construction trades, longshoring, and barbering, and were crowded into the menial and low-wage occupations in which they are now found. When industry developed, blacks were largely excluded from the factory jobs except at the lowest custodial level. For example, this happened in the steel industry in Birmingham and in textiles and furniture manufacturing in the Carolinas. Opportunities that might have broken the grip of sharecropping in the rural South more rapidly were closed off in the cities by restricting higher paying jobs to whites and crowding blacks into a relatively few menial occupations.

Similar developments occurred in the North during and after the First World War I. The black migration to northern cities led to the closing of some occupations to blacks in which they had already found a strong foothold and to their restriction to menial occupations. This form of economic exploitation was accompanied by residential segregation; restrictive covenants in real estate deeds and residential zoning as means of exclusion of people from specific

[11]C. Vann Woodward, *The Strange Career of Jim Crow* (New York: Oxford University Press, 1955), is the standard treatment of the rapid spread of Jim Crow laws and disfranchisement of blacks during the 1890s in the South. Woodward, however, failed to note the importance of the black migration to cities and gave inadequate attention to the changes in occupations and economic opportunity that occurred.

neighborhoods were first used on a large scale in the 1920s. Loss of the franchise and pervasive Jim Crow legislation were never a major feature of the northern reaction, but the results were similar. A pattern of coerced labor based on tradition, custom, and the attitudes of white workers and employers emerged, enforced in part by labor unions but more rigidly by customary practices in the labor market and the educational system. At the root of the problem are the forces described in the last chapter that create and sustain the ghetto economy and its force of low-wage labor. Coercion of that portion of the labor force depends not on law, but is built into the structure and functioning of the economy as a whole.

This brief economic history of the black worker in America indicates that the form of coerced labor has changed, but that the coercion has persisted. The intensity of exploitation diminished but the fact remains that blacks have been kept in a disadvantaged position. They are no longer property. They are no longer held in thrall by a combination of economic circumstance and legal constraint. But they are oppressed by an economic system which largely relegates them to crowded occupations and low wage jobs.

Crowding and Economic Opportunity

The 1960s witnessed a significant increase in the number of blacks in higher level occupations. Between 1960 and 1969 the number of black men over 25 in professional and technical occupations increased by 107 percent. In managerial occupations the number increased by 117 percent. Other large increases occurred in employment as craftsmen (52 percent) and salesmen (42 percent). All of these percentage increases were greater than the percent increase of black men over 25 in the labor force as a whole. These data may indicate a widening of opportunities for blacks, under the impact of rising prosperity, pressure from the federal government, black militancy, and general agitation for fair treatment for blacks. How far this development will go remains to be seen, particularly since rising prosperity was replaced by recession in 1970-1971, and some union resistance to affirmative action hiring programs has developed. Nevertheless, many commentators point to these developments as indicating a major breakthrough for minority groups in the opportunity system.

That optimism may not be justified. It is quite possible for new opportunities to be opened for minority groups, while the bulk of the minority remains crowded into menial occupations. The significant changes that would indicate a new pattern of opportunity would be a shift of the white majority into menial occupations and of racial minority groups out of them. We can claim that crowding has stopped and discrimination is eliminated when the proportion of blacks in menial occupations, corrected for educational qualifications, is no larger than the proportion of blacks in the labor force.

Barbara Bergmann and other researchers in her Research Project on the Economics of Discrimination at the University of Maryland have been able to show a systematic relationship between the proportion of blacks in the population of urban areas and the proportion of the labor force in menial occupations. Menial occupations are defined as those in which a majority of the workers are not high school graduates. Using data from U.S. metropolitan areas, the Bergmann researchers found the following relationship:

$$M = 9 + .09x$$

where M = the percent of the labor force in menial occupations, and
   x = the percent of blacks in the population.

That is, if there were no blacks in the population, 9 percent of the labor force would be employed in menial occupations. For every 1 percent increase of blacks in the population there would be a 9/100ths of 1 percent increase in the proportion of the labor force employed in menial occupations. Thus, if 10 percent of the population were black, 9.9 percent of the labor force would be employed in menial occupations:

$$\begin{aligned} M &= 9 + .09x \\ &= 9 + .09(10) \\ &= 9 + .9 \\ &= 9.9 \end{aligned}$$

Figure 5.4 shows this relationship graphically. The diagram also includes the proportion of blacks in the labor force (L), which is assumed to be the same as the proportion of blacks in the total population.

Figure 5.4 is quite revealing. As a model of the labor market it can illustrate the pure effects of crowding, unmodified by any other considerations. If we start from the origin, an urban metropolitan area with no blacks will have 9 percent of its workers employed in

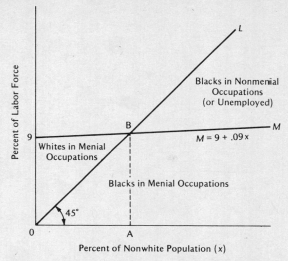

M = Percent of the labor force employed in menial occupations
L = Nonwhite percent of the labor force (assumed to equal the
percent of nonwhitespopulation).

FIGURE 5.4 Relationship between Black Population and Employment in Menial Occupations.

menial occupations. As the proportion of blacks in the popula tion
increases, so does the proportion of blacks in the labor force (L).
They are crowded into the menial occupations while the number of
whites employed in those occupations falls. When the percentage of
blacks in the population rises to 0A the entire black work force is
employed in menial occupations and no whites hold those types of
jobs. If the proportion of blacks in the population continues to
increase, one of three things can occur:

1. Some of the additional black workers will be unemployed. The
increase in jobs in the menial occupations is too small to absorb all
of the additional black workers, and enemployment rates for blacks
will rise. This effect of crowding helps to explain the very high
unemployment rates found in urban ghettos.

2. Some formerly all-white occupations may be redefined as
menial occupations and add to the employment opportunities for
blacks. This change would be equivalent to an upward shift of M in
Figure 5.4.

3. Some blacks will find employment in "white" nonmenial occupations, even though the menial occupations remain all black. It is quite possible for blacks to move into such occupational categories as managerial, professional, and technical, crafts, and sales without significantly modifying the process by which the bulk of the black labor force is crowded into menial occupations.

No one would argue that this pure model of crowding corresponds with reality in all details. Reality is far more complex and varied. But the analytical model can show the direction of trends in the real world. In particular, it alerts us anew to the problem of employment of minority groups in the low-wage menial occupations as an essential element of discrimination in the labor market. Hiring black college professors, for example, does not by itself significantly modify the coercion of the black labor force into menial occupations.

Lack of alternative opportunities is the chief economic factor that preserves the pattern of coerced labor. A thoroughgoing opening of employment opportunities to minority groups should have the effect, in the long run, of eroding the labor market patterns that result in crowding. It is for this reason that fair employment legislation and affirmative action programs are so important. Combined with improved education, manpower training, and related programs, they could ultimately end the conditions that lead to economic coercion of minority groups in the labor force. This optimism must be qualified by caution, however. Little progress can be made if opportunities for minority groups are opened up more slowly than the proportionate increase of the minority groups in the labor force. If that were the case, crowding would persist and coercion of labor for the great bulk of the workers from minority groups would remain. Unless there is a shift of coerced labor out of menial occupations, movement of some into high-level jobs will not be very meaningful.

CHAPTER 6

Welfare Payments and the Ghetto Economy

On Thanksgiving Day—the festival of the bountiful board—in 1969 in Louisville, Kentucky, a 10-year-old boy died of starvation. The next day the newspapers carried stories asking how such a thing could happen in the middle of a big city in modern America. The answer was not hard to find, although neither of the local newspapers was able to identify it. The boy was one of a family group of 7 persons receiving welfare payments of $179 per month. That averages out to about 86 cents per day per person for food, clothing, shelter, and all other expenses.

An eighth person was also a member of the family group, the father of several of the children. He earned from $4 to $10 per day, he said, repairing small electrical equipment. Even if he averaged about $7 per day for 6 days a week, this would raise the income per person per day to only about $1.06.

Perhaps it is possible to survive on these amounts. But in this case one child starved to death and all the other children suffered from malnutrition. At the very best, this family was surviving at the lowest levels of poverty. The development of the children was severely hampered, and their poverty was being preserved not only for the present generation, but for the future as well. The head of the local welfare agency attributed the death to "irresponsible parents."

The Inadequacy of Welfare Payments

Although individual cases like the one just described are well known to welfare personnel and the general inadequacy of welfare payments is acknowledged, estimates of just how far welfare payments fall below acceptable standards have seldom been made. Yet such estimates are relatively easy to make. For example, the estimate that follows was made for 1968, using only data available at that time in order to show the information accessible to policy makers and how it might be used.

The most widely accepted standard for adequacy of family income is the so-called "poverty line" established by the Social Security Administration and calculated by Mollie Orshansky. It is based on the cost of the economy food plan devised by the U. S. Department of Agriculture (USDA). This cost is multiplied by three, using the ratio of food to total expenditures which prevailed in low-income budgets in 1958. The resulting poverty benchmark for a nonfarm family of four was $3,335 per year in 1966. On a monthly basis it was $277.90.[1]

Many doubts about this poverty line can be raised. The USDA economy food plan may not be fully adequate, and it requires a sophisticated knowledge of both diets and buying that the poor do not have. In addition, budget patterns have changed since 1958. Among low-income families the proportion of income spent on food was closer to one-quarter than to one-third in 1968, largely because of increases in prices of other budget items relative to the price of food. Under these conditions a budget based on a 3 to 1 ratio of total expenditures to food would leave serious inadequacies in the total. Although the "Orshansky line" is widely used, its meagerness is recognized by its originator and by most of those who use it as a standard.

A second estimate of the poverty line is available. The Bureau of Labor Statistics (BLS) developed a low cost budget described as the amount needed to provide an urban family of four with a minimally adequate standard of nutrition, medical care, and housing. The cost of that budget for 1967 was $4,862 or $405.17 per month. Yet even this level was qualified by the statement that "although possible to achieve nutritional adequacy from the low cost plan . . . only one-fourth of those spending this amount do obtain adequate diets."[2] According to this second estimate, which was admittedly minimal, it took 46 percent more money than the generally accepted Orshansky line for an urban family of four to escape poverty.

Both of these estimates will be used here to measure the adequacy of payments under the program of Aid to Families with Dependent Children (AFDC) in 1968. We use 1968 for several reasons. The situation in that year shows the more normal pattern of welfare payments prior to the great increases of 1969-1971, which probably reflected the use of welfare payments as a means of social control following the riots in the cities. We shall argue later that welfare payments are always used as a means of social control, but the 1969-1971 levels represent a special situation resulting from extraordinary social strains and conflict. Although the great urban riots occurred in the 1965-1967 period, the slow-moving welfare bureaucracy did not respond with significantly enlarged payments

[1]Mollie Orshansky, "Shape of Poverty in 1966," Social Security Bulletin (March 1968), pp. 5-6.
[2]Three Standards of Living for an Urban Family of Four Persons, Bulletin No. 15705, U. S. Department of Labor, Bureau of Labor Statistics (Washington: 1967).

and wider eligibility (except in New York) until the last years of the decade. The year 1968 may be taken, then, as typical of the situation out of which the riots emerged.

Welfare Payments and Poverty in 1968

AFDC payments in 1968 raised the average family income of recipients to a level equal to about half of the poverty income. The average size of the AFDC family unit will be taken as four, since the ratio of total AFDC recipients to the number of AFDC families was 3.997.[3] This ratio is fairly constant for individual states as well; therefore, it is appropriate to use the poverty lines that have been computed for a family of four.

The estimates have been made in the following fashion: We started with the average monthly AFDC payment per family for December 1968. The average family income per month from other sources was then added to the monthly AFDC payment. The most recent available data was for 1961, and it had to be updated. This was done by increasing the 1961 amounts by 50 percent, which is approximately equal to the increase in personal income per capita for the U.S. between 1961 and 1968. This figure is probably a good estimate. The 50 percent increase is somewhat high for Michigan but low for Illinois in 1958, according to preliminary data from the 1968 Survey of Welfare Recipients. In any case, the error will be small because income from other sources than AFDC payments is usually a small portion of the total.[4]

After computing the total monthly income from AFDC plus other sources, we subtracted it from the poverty line incomes, first the Orshansky line of $277.90 per month and then the BLS line of $305.17 per month. The remainder was the unmet need per month per family.

This figure was multiplied by the number of families receiving AFDC payments in December 1968 to obtain the total unmet need per

[3]"Program and Operating Statistics," *Welfare in Review* (U. S. Department Health, Education and Welfare, Social and Rehabilitation Service), Vol. 7, No. 3 (May-June 1969), p. 38.

[4]In 1961 only 19.1 percent of all support for AFDC recipients came from sources other than welfare. This percent includes OASDI payments as well as other sources of income. U. S. Department of Health, Education and Welfare, Welfare Administration, Bureau of Family Services, Division of Program Statistics and Analysis, *Characteristics of Families Receiving AFDC*, April 1963, Table 39.

month, which was then multiplied by 12 to obtain the annual unmet need for a 12-month period.

The results are given in Table 6.1, which shows the unmet needs of welfare recipients in 1968 to have been about $1.27 billion based on the Orshansky poverty line and about $3.60 billion based on the BLS poverty line.

TABLE 6.1

Estimated Unmet Income Needs of Welfare (AFDC) Recipients, 1968

Average monthly AFDC payment per family[a]	$167.80
Average monthly income from other sources[b] × 1.5	$ 40.25
Average total income per AFDC family	$208.05
Monthly unmet need per family based on	
Orshansky line ($277.90 per month)	$ 69.85
BLS line ($405.17 per month)	$197.12
Number of recipient families[a]	1,521,000
Annual unmet need for all recipient familes, 1968, based on	
Orshansky line ($3,335)	$1,274,000,000
BLS line ($4,862)	$3,597,000,000

[a]*Welfare in Review,* Vol. 7, No. 3 (May-June 1969), p. 38.
[b]U. S. Department of Health, Education and Welfare, *Characteristics of Families Receiving AFDC* (April 1963), Table 48.

The significance of these figures can be indicated by comparing them with total AFDC expenditures of a little less than $2.9 billion in 1968. Bringing that total up to the Orshansky line would have raised it to over $4.1 billion. The BLS poverty line would have more than doubled the total to $6.5 billion, Yet only the *existing* recipients would have been covered. Those eligible but not receiving assistance are not included in these estimates.

The total cost of AFDC would have been doubled if those eligible for assistance but not receiving it were included. Administrative restrictions, lack of knowledge by potential recipients, and social pressures tend to reduce the number of persons receiving AFDC payments to about half of those who need them and are eligible. If that large group were included the total 1968 cost of AFDC based on the Orshansky line would have been about $8.25 billion, and based on the BLS line it would have come to about $13 billion. These figures compare with the actual expenditures of $2.9 billion in 1968.

It might be argued that these results obscure the differences between states, and indeed they do. Nevertheless, only four states provided AFDC payments large enough to bring total income for AFDC families above the Orshansky poverty line. These four were Massachusetts, Connecticut, New York, and New Jersey. Together they accounted for 355,000 AFDC families, or 23 percent of the total. No state provided a level of AFDC support high enough to bring the average AFDC family up to the BLS poverty line.

Social and Economic Impact of Welfare

Many studies of the welfare system link the low level of AFDC payments to the perpetuation of dependency and the continuation of poverty. One study argued that payments providing barely adequate amounts for food and shelter create conditions of "anxiety, isolation and hopelessness." An evaluation of AFDC in Chicago pointed out that payments are not sufficient for "reasonable subsistence compatible with health and well-being." This deprivation "sets the ADC child apart and handicaps his ability to grow up like the other children in the community." The budget standard "is so low that it interferes with efforts to help families achieve personal and economic independence." Another study argued that welfare recipients are handicapped in taking advantage of betterment programs: "When people are sick and hungry and live under demoralizing, degrading conditions, they cannot make use of opportunities or services that might ultimately lift them out of their poverty."[5]

Studies by Greenleigh Associates in New York State, Detroit, and the state of Washington all point to the perpetuation of dependency and poverty through welfare payments. In New York the welfare

[5]Peter S. Albin and Bruno Stein, "The Constrained Demand for Public Assistance," *Journal of Human Resources*, Vol. 3, No. 3 (Summer 1968), pp. 300-311; Frances Fox Piven and Richard A. Cloward, *Regulating the Poor: The Functions of Public Welfare* (New York: Pantheon Books, 1971), pp. 160, 217-219; Gil Bonem and Philip Reno, "By Bread Alone, and Little Bread: Life on ADC," *Social Work*, Vol. 13, No. 4 pp. 5-11; Welfare Council of Metropolitan Chicago, *ADC: Facts, Fallacies, Future: Summary of a Study of the ADC Program in Cook County* (Chicago: 1962), pp. 18-20; Bernice Madison, "The Response of Public Welfare to the Challenge of Social and Economic Opportunity," *Public Welfare*, Vol. 24, No. 4 (Oct. 1966), pp. 306-319.

system "shows little regard for them [recipients] as human beings, defeats their attempts to regain self-esteem and self-direction, and tends to prolong the duration of dependency." In the Midwest the welfare program in Detroit "tends to perpetuate dependency by inadequate grants and confusing, inefficient organization." On the Pacific coast in Washington "present standards of assistance tend to pauperize public assistance recipients . . . families tend to deteriorate . . . may have debilitating effects on the recipients."[6]

The National Advisory Commission on Civil Disorders has charged the welfare system with contributing to tension and social disorder, encouraging dependency, alienating the recipient, and undermining self-respect. The Citizens Board of Inquiry into Hunger and Malnutrition concluded that "welfare is at best irrational. At its worst—as is most often the case—it is an unrelenting assault on family integrity and stability." Daniel Moynihan argues that the system "maintains the poverty groups in society in a position of impotent fury. Impotent because the system destroys the potential of individuals and families to improve themselves. Fury because it claims to be otherwise."[7]

In one respect, the welfare economy is notorious. Administration of the welfare system has been blamed for a serious deterioration in the family structure. By withholding payments from families with an able-bodied male worker, the system encourages the unemployed man to desert his family in order for them to receive assistance. The welfare system has undoubtedly had that effect, but other aspects of the ghetto economy work in the same direction, including low wages, erratic employment, and general conditions of poverty. Family stability is discouraged by the difficulties that poverty brings. Desertion has always been the poor man's divorce.[8]

The welfare economy discourages people on welfare from work-

[6]Greenleigh Associates, Inc., *Report to the Moreland Commission on Welfare of the Findings of the Study of the Public Assistance Programs and Operations of the State of New York* (New York: Greenleigh Associates, 1964), p. 3; *Study of Services to Deal with Poverty in Detroit, Michigan* (New York: Greenleigh Associates, 1965), pp. 37-47; *Poverty-Prevention or Perpetuation: A Study of the State Department of Public Assistance of the State of Washington, Summary Report* (New York: Greenleigh Associates, 1964), pp. 6, 20, 23.

[7]*Report of the National Advisory Commission on Civil Disorders* (Washington: U.S. Government Printing Office, 1968), pp. 252-256; Citizens Board of Inquiry Into Hunger and Malnutrition in the United States, *Hunger, U.S.A.* (Washington: New Community Press, 1968) p. 70; Daniel Moynihan, "The Crisis in Welfare," The *Public Interest*, No. 10 (Winter 1968), pp. 3-29.

[8]See Kenneth B. Clark, "Sex, Status and Underemployment of the Negro Male" in A. M. Ross and Herbert Hill (eds.), *Employment, Race and Poverty* (New York: Harcourt Brace Jovanovich, 1967), for an analysis of the relationship between economic factors and Negro family stability. Also, *The Negro Family* (The "Moynihan Report"), Office of Policy Planning and Research (Washington: U. S. Department of Labor, March 1965).

ing. Until 1969 earnings were usually deducted in full from the welfare payment. Since working also involves expenses (travel, clothes, and so forth), the welfare recipient who worked frequently ended up worse off than if he did not work. The 1969 changes in federal legislation have reduced this "100 percent tax" on earnings to about 65 percent. A family on welfare can avoid these effects only by breaking the law. Many do that, bringing about further disintegration of social controls and decreased respect for the institutions of organized society. Efforts to "beat the system" are generated by the system itself. Welfare recipients sometimes work and do not report their income, the husband appears to leave the family but actually does not, and relatives sometimes provide unreported financial assistance. The social worker and welfare administrator are then obliged to become investigators and adversaries rather than helpers, establishing a conflict relationship between themselves and the welfare families.

The welfare system institutionalizes poverty and dependence. Although any one family may receive welfare payments for a relatively short period of time, the system as a whole continues indefinitely, sustaining a group of welfare recipients whose membership may be in flux but which persists as a group. "Our present policy of dealing with poverty is designed not to eliminate, but to institutionalize it," according to Robert Hess, who argues that ' we are in the process of creating a permanent 'welfare class' . . . within a publicly financed bureaucratic structure." The system is "analagous to colonialism," according to Glenn Jacobs, creating "a state of unilateral dependence, labeling and maintaining the individual in the socially defined category of the poor."[9]

It is evident that the welfare economy has a perverse effect on the ghetto economy. It encourages family disintegration, discourages work, and promotes a breakdown of social controls. These long-run effects may well be more costly than the short-run gains obtained by seeing that needy people receive the nominally necessary food, clothing and shelter. The level of welfare payments keeps the recipients in poverty. Their poverty, in turn, tends to reinforce itself because of the social and psychological impact of poverty upon the poor.

[9]Robert D. Hess, "Educability and Rehabilitation: The Future of the Welfare Class," *Journal of Marriage and the Family*, Vol. 26, No. 4 (Nov. 1964), pp. 422-429; Glenn Jacobs, "The Reification of the Notion of Subculture in Public Welfare," *Social Casework*, Vol. 49, No. 9 (Nov. 1968), pp. 527-534.

Expansion of the Welfare System

A steady upswing in the size of the U.S. public assistance system began during the latter part of World War II. Just as economic growth has brought a higher GNP, increased output of goods and services, and rising prices, it has also brought an increased number of persons receiving public assistance and increased spending for that purpose. As the economy progressed, poverty became more heavily institutionalized.

In 1945 four public assistance programs were in operation: old-age assistance, aid to the blind, AFDC, and general assistance. The first three were federal programs and the last primarily local. In that year the total expenditures for the four programs was $990 million, and some 3,085,000 persons were served. The breakdown of recipients and expenditures by program is shown in Table 6.2.

Almost a quarter century later, in 1970, the number of public assistance programs had doubled. Aid to the permanently and totally disabled began in 1950, medical assistance for the aged in 1960, medical assistance for the poor in 1966, and emergency assistance in 1968. There has also been a tremendous increase in both recipients and payments. The situation in 1969 and June 1970 is shown in Table 6.3.

Comparison of the public assistance programs in 1945 and 1970 shows almost no change in the number of persons receiving old-age assistance and aid to the blind and a moderate increase in persons receiving general assistance, although the total payments have followed the cost of living upward and a little more. The largest

TABLE 6.2

Public Assistance Programs, 1945

	RECIPIENTS (THOUSANDS)	TOTAL PAYMENTS (MILLIONS OF $)
Old-age assistance	2,056	726.6
Aid to the blind	71	26.6
AFDC	701[a]	149.7
General assistance	257	86.9
Total	3,085	989.7

[a] Includes only children

TABLE 6.3

Public Assistance Programs, 1969 and June 1970

PROGRAM	1969		JUNE 1970	
	RECIPIENTS (THOUSANDS	TOTAL PAYMENTS (MILLIONS OF $)	RECIPIENTS (THOUSANDS)	TOTAL PAYMENTS (MILLIONS OF $)
Old-age assistance (OAA)	2,077	1,747	2,052	153.4
Aid to the blind (AB)	81	91	80	8.2
Aid to the permenently and totally disabled (APTD)	803	787	874	82.6
Aid to families with dependent children (AFDC)		3,533		391.2
Families	1,875		2,158	
Children	5,413		6,091	
Children and adults	7,313		8,291	
General assistance	857	475	926	49.9
Total	11,131	6,866	12,233	685.3

SOURCE: *Social Security Bulletin*, Annual Statistical Supplement (1969), p. 132; *Welfare in Review*, Vol. 8, No. 6 (November–December 1970), p. 28.

increases among persons served are in AFDC—up from 701,000 to almost 8,300,000—and aid to the disabled—from no program to over 870,000 recipients. The largest increases in cost have been in AFDC—from about $150 million to over $3.5 billion (about $4.7 billion an annual basis by June 1970)—and in medicare's more than $5.6 billion, much of which has gone to the group receiving AFDC.

But medicare does not provide continuing family support. AFDC does. It supports over 8 million persons in poverty and provides over $4.5 billion in income for that purpose. Furthermore, the number of persons supported by AFDC has marched steadily upward to present levels, with substantial acceleration in the growth trend in recent years. This growth is shown in Figure 6.1.

The growth in AFDC expenditures went through three stages. From 1946 through 1949 payments rose from about $15 million to about $45 million each month—partly because the economy returned to peacetime activity, partly because of the post-World War II inflation, and partly because adults in the family became eligible for assistance, There followed six years of stability into the mid-1950s. The second stage of increasing AFDC payments begain in 1956, when the great expansion of the urban ghettos began to be felt. It was inevitable that the welfare caseload should rise. The poverty, unemployment, and disintegration of family life characteristic of the urban ghetto could lead to nothing else. The riots of 1967-1968 led to the third stage, an acceleration of the increase to reach the high levels of the early 1970s of over $400 million per month.

The rapid acceleration of AFCD expenditures that began in the mid-1960s coincided with the urban riots of 1964-1968. One of the reactions of the social order to those revolts was to alleviate tensions and reduce discontent by admitting more persons to eligibility for AFDC and by raising payments.[10] Much of the campaign against poverty had the same effects. The welfare system first resisted the increased need: the great black migration of the first half of the 1950s brought almost no response, for total AFDC payments re-

[10]See Frances Fox Piven and Richard A. Cloward, *Regulating the Poor: The Functions of Public Welfare* (New York: Pantheon Books, 1971), Ch. 6-10 for a detailed analysis of the welfare "explosion" of the 1960s as a response to the urban revolt. A more orthodox view of the increase in welfare payments was expressed by David M. Gordon, "Income and Welfare in New York City," *The Public Interest*, No. 16 (Summer 1969), pp. 64-88: "One can easily argue that the cause of the welfare "crisis is simply the widespread poverty in the city—not chiseling or welfare rights organizations or liberal administrative practices," p. 87.

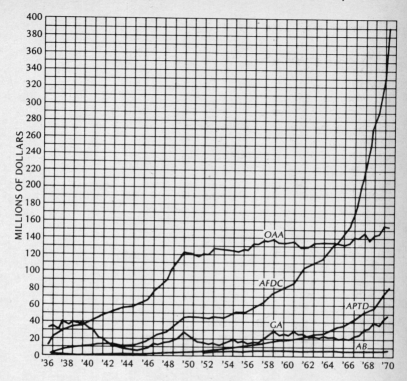

FIGURE 6.1 Public Assistance Money Payments by Program, June and December Each Year, 1936 to 1969

SOURCE: Welfare in Review, Vol. 8, No. 1 (January-February 1970), p. 43; No. 3 (May-June 1970), p. 25; No. 6 (November-December 1970), p. 28.

mained level until about 1956-1957. Then, reluctantly, the system began to accommodate itself to increased needs, with a steady increase in total payments to mid-1966. At that time the need to defuse the black revolt brught huge increases in welfare payments that lasted into the early 1970s. By late 1971 the administration of the welfare system began to clamp down and stopped the increases—a sure sign that the urban revolt of the mid-1960s had ended in failure.

The Role of Welfare Payments

When David Caplovitz surveyed a sample of residents of four low-income housing projects in 1960 in New York City, he found that 28 percent of the sample received incomes wholly or partly from welfare or pensions.[11] The proportion would certainly be higher today. In 1968 almost one million persons in New York City were receiving public assistance payments alone, or about 12 percent of the population of the city as a whole. In 1960 the number receiving public assistance (not pensions) was around 375,000.

A November 1966 survey of slum areas in major U.S. cities showed that 47 percent of the families in the survey received transfer payments, including unemployment insurance (5.1 percent), welfare or AFDC (18.1 percent), and other nonemployment income (24.6 percent). In the slums of Los Angeles 30 percent of the population received welfare payments, and in Cleveland 21 percent of the families received AFDC payments. In all of the areas surveyed a very large proportion of the city's welfare cases were slum residents.

Welfare payments perform some significant functions in the ghetto economy. Their most important role is the preservation of the ghetto economy itself. There is a continuous drain of resources and income out of the ghetto which normally would set in motion a downward spiral of incomes and economic activity until the economic subsystem of the ghetto stabilized itself at a very low level. This "normal" equilibrium, so to speak, could be sustained by the inflow of incomes to the ghetto by way of employment in the low-wage industries and other inflows of earned income and transfer payments. At this lower equilibrium level we would expect the ghetto economy to support a smaller irregular economy, the pool of low-wage labor would be larger, and higher rates of unemployment would prevail. The extent and depths of poverty would be vastly greater than they are now.

It is welfare payments that enable the economic equilibrium of the urban ghetto to be sustained at a somewhat higher level. The income transfers from the progressive sector of the economy, which welfare payments represent, increase the total income of the ghetto, support a larger irregular economy, and enable the ghetto subsystem to function at a somewhat higher level than its "normal" equilibrium. For example, welfare payments enable a larger number of family units to subsist at the poverty level. These family units add to the

[11] See David Caplovitz, The Poor Pay More: Consumer Practices of Low Income Families (New York: Free Press, 1967).

demand for slum housing from the housing industry.[12] The net result is a larger ghetto area and a larger outflow of physical capital into the hands of slumlords. By contrast, if there were no welfare payments, the families now receiving them would either perish or double up with related persons into even larger family units. The demand for slum housing would be smaller and the ghettos themselves would be reduced in size. But population densities would be greater, incomes would be lower (per person), and the conditions of poverty would be intensified.

It is important to note, however, that while welfare payments are able to raise the incomes of the recipient families, and thereby reduce the intensity of poverty within the ghetto as a whole, the drain of resources and income out of the ghetto continues. Those property owners and businessmen who make profits out of the ghetto are expanded in numbers, and their receipts are enlarged. This is the fundamental dilemma faced by public policies that seek to ameliorate the condition of ghetto residents: while they may succeed in improving conditions of life for the recipients, they also result n preservation of the ghetto as a whole.

As long as welfare payments are so low that they keep recipients mired in poverty, any given level of payments will serve to stabilize the urban ghettos at a particular level of existence. Lower welfare payments will mean a greater degree of poverty there, while higher payments will mean poverty of less intensity. But whatever the level, *the function of welfare payments in the social system as a whole is to preserve the urban ghetto and its supply of low wage labor.* When unrest and turmoil reach high levels we can expect one reaction to be an increase in welfare payments that has the effect of stabilizing the social order. The "Law of Welfare Payments" is the following: welfare payments will be set at that level which enables law and order to be maintained by the ordinary instruments of social control.

Welfare Reform

Major proposals for "reform" of the welfare system were presented to Congress by President Nixon in 1969. After intensive

[12]See Richard F. Muth, *Cities and Housing: The Spatial Pattern of Urban Residential Land Use* (Chicago: University of Chicago Press, 1969), pp. 14, 115-135, and 241-283. Public subsidy to slums through AFDC payments is also suggested in Alice R. McCabe, "Forty Forgotten Families," *Public Welfare*, Vol. 24, No. 2 (April 1966), pp. 159-171, esp. p. 164.

debate and revision in Congress the Nixon plan (called the Family Assistance Plan) was rejected in the final days of the 1972 session. The essential elements of the major legislation proposed by the administration follow:

1. There would have been a national cash income floor of $2,400 a year for dependent families of four.

2. The employed poor would be eligible for assistance. Earnings of $700 a year plus a small allowance for work expenses and child care would bring no reduction in welfare payments. All amounts earned above $700 would reduce welfare payments by two-thirds of the amount above $700. For example, earnings of $2,000 above the work expenses allotment would reduce the welfare payment from $2,400 to $1,533, giving a family income of $3,533. When a family of four earned $4,300 above the allowance for work expenses, it would receive no welfare assistance.

3. Stringent work requirements would be imposed on welfare recipients, requiring that they accept appropriate work at $1.20 per hour. The work requirement applied to mothers in fatherless families, even though the legislation did not make adequate provision for day care facilities.

4. Provision was made for 200,000 temporary public service jobs, and other proposed legislation would have made available another 200,000.

5. Eligibility requirements were sharply stiffened in a variety of ways, including what would be, in effect, a nine-month waiting period for some families and permanent ineligibility for many seasonal and migrant workers.

The proposed Family Assistance Plan would have covered about 5 million families, or some 25 million people, of whom 16 million were children and some 9 million adults. Three million of the families would have been two-parent families in which one or both parents work—the working poor. Some 70 percent of these families are white, and about 50 percent have annual incomes less than $1000. The other 2 million families were those headed by women. The entire program would have been accomplished with an increase in costs of $4.4 billion annually, in addition to the $10 billion spent on public assistance in 1970 by the federal and state governments.[13]

[13]On the proposed Family Assistance Plan, see President's Commission on Income Maintenance Programs, *Poverty Amid Plenty: The American Paradox* (Washington: U.S. Government Printing Office, November 1969); U.S. Congress, House of Representatives Committee on Ways and Means, *The President's Proposals for Welfare Reforms and Social Security Amendments* (Washington, U.S. Government Printing Office, October

In one sense this welfare reform proposal represented a major change in the program. It recognized a national standard for a minimum family income, even though the minimum of $2,400 was far below the 1970 poverty income for a family of four of $3,968 (estimated by the Orshansky method). Many liberals argued that it was the establishment of the principle that was important and that the minimum could be raised later. Skeptics argued that it was far more likely that the poverty level would rise because of inflation while the government's minimum family income lagged behind. That has been the history of minima in the case of unemployment insurance and social security benefits.

In another sense, the legislation was a step backward because of its stiffening of eligibility requirements. For example, it would discourage recipients from seeking a hearing before their grants are terminated, and it required a personal investigation of each applicant instead of permitting eligibility on the basis of an affidavit of need. These and similar provisions reduce the dignity and privacy of welfare recipients more than the present system does and preserve the large and costly bureaucracy needed for administration.

Potentially, the worst aspects of the legislation were the provisions relating to the working poor. Although welfare recipients could improve their incomes by work, after they earn the first $700 above the allowance for work expenses, they would lose $2 from their welfare payment for every $3 they earn. This was equivalent to a marginal income tax rate of 66 2/3 percent, which was a higher rate than that paid by the very affluent. The work incentive was very weak.

The unemployed poor would have been required to work at a wage rate of $1.20 per hour, which was well below the national minimum wage. A provision of this sort would have the effect of creating a permanent low-wage labor force for the many types of employment not covered by minimum wage laws. It would also act as a general depressant for wage rates at or above the minimum because of the existence of a large group of workers who are forced to work for less than the minimum.

1969); *ibid., Family Assistance Act of 1970, Report on H.R. 16311* (Washington: U.S. Government Printing Office, 1970); U.S. Congress, Senate Finance Committee, *Hearings, Family Assistance Act of 1970* (Washington: Government Printing Office, 1970).

Several short critiques of FAP discuss its economic impact: Edith G. Levi, "Mr. Nixon's Speenhamland," *Social Work*, Vol. 15, No. 1 (Jan. 1970), pp. 7-11; William W. Taylor, "Unintended Consequences of the Nixon Welfare Plan," *ibid.*, Vol 15, No. 4 (Oct. 1970), pp. 15-22; Sydney E. Bernard, "The Nixon Family Assistance Plan: How It Will Fail and Why I Support It," *Poverty and Human Resources*, Vol. 5, No. 5 (Sept.-Oct. 1970), pp. 5-13.

Finally, the legislation would have created a substantial "Speenhamland effect" in labor markets. That phrase takes its name from a similar program of aid to the working poor instituted in England in 1798, during a period in which wages were too low to provide a minimum subsistence income for low-wage workers and their families. A group of justices of the peace meeting at Speenhamland, in southern England, agreed upon a sliding scale of "relief in aid of wages" designed to bring family incomes for the working poor up to the subsistence level. The results were disastrous. Employers had every incentive to drive wages down, thereby shifting the burden of supporting the worker to the taxpayer. Workers had no opportunity to get more than a bare subsistence income. Morale broke down, and an era of high absenteeism, low productivity, drunkenness, and broken families followed. Many of the worst aspects of the early industrial revolution in England can be traced to the Speenhamland system of relief payments to the working poor.

Although the Nixon welfare reform legislation differed somewhat from the Speenhamland system, it would have produced some of the same effects. If enacted as proposed, it would have institutionalized the poverty that results from low-wage employment. It would have created a permanent labor force of workers employed below the minimum wage. It provided weak incentives to the worker who would like to increase his income. And it encouraged employers to hold wage rates down and shift as much of their labor costs as they could to the federal taxpayer. In its long-range effects on the labor market the so-called welfare "reform" could create a major disaster for the American worker, and particularly for those in low-wage employment.

The apparent benefits masked a program that would freeze a large supply of low-wage workers into the labor market and solidify a hard core of poverty into the American social and economic system. It was a prescription for permanent poverty. Yet the ideas behind the Nixon welfare reform proposals are not dead. The idea that welfare payments should be tied to a work requirement continues to be popular; however, its long-term effects are poorly understood. The present welfare system already has a Work Incentive Program (WIN) that enables welfare recipients who are able to do so to work in public service and other jobs. Although that program is still in the experimental stage, it already shows some of the "Speenhamland effect" described above.[14]

[14]A series of studies of the Michigan experience with employment programs for welfare recipients show initial effects that include increased numbers of persons receiving welfare payments and higher costs to the public. See Robert F. Schlenker, Ronald E. Fine, and Gary L. Appel, *AFDC Employment Incentives: Economic Implications of the New Income Disregard Provisions and the Proposed Nixon Reforms* (Lansing: State of Michigan Department of Social Services, 1970); Vernon K. Smith and Aydia Ulusan, *The Employment of AFDC Recipients in Michigan* (Lansing: State of Michigan Department of Social Services, 1972); Ronald E. Fine and others, *Final Report: AFDC Employment and Referral Guidelines* (Lansing: State of Michigan Department of Social Services, 1972); Gary L. Appel, *Effects of a Financial Incentive on AFDC Employment: Michigan's Experience Between July 1969 and July 1970* (Minneapolis: Institute for Interdisciplinary Studies, 1972).

CHAPTER 7

Business Enterprise in the Urban Ghetto

The retail business districts of central city ghettos present an outward appearance much like any retail district, except that they are usually a little shabbier and obviously cater primarily to a low-income clientele. There are important differences that are not obvious to the casual observer, however. Business practices are exploitive, and the customers often have few, if any, alternative sources of supply. In addition, the racial composition of the ghetto has tended to create a partially segregated, black retail market.

The underworld of shady and often unethical business enterprise which flourishes in the urban ghetto has been studied and described in depth by David Caplovitz, whose book illustrates the extent to which a distinct business way of life flourishes in the relatively isolated markets of central city poverty areas.[1] Retail firms, particularly those selling consumer durables, prosper through provision of easy credit, selling high-priced and often shoddy merchandise by use of high-pressure tactics, and personal methods of attracting customers and getting payment. Door-to-door peddling is common. This system of business enterprise is highly exploitive; high prices, high cost of credit, and shabby merchandise effectively strip the poor of whatever assets they may have and ensure their continuation in poverty. These practices are often supplemented by use of the law courts to get payment; repossession and garnishment of wages are devices used by furniture, appliance, and jewelry stores in particular. Business practices of the ghetto perform an important function in the

---

[1]David Caplovitz, *The Poor Pay More: Consumer Practices of Low Income Families* (New York: Free Press, 1967). Other sources for inner city business practices include:

Frederick D. Sturdivant (ed.), *The Ghetto as Marketplace* (New York: Free Press, 1969), especially the articles by Louise G. Richards, "Consumer Practices of the Poor" and Mary Gardiner Jones, "Deception in the Marketplace of the Poor: The Role of the Federal Trade Commission." This volume also contains the Federal Trade Commission "Economic Report on Installment Credit and Retail Sales Practices of District of Columbia Retailers."

Charles S. Goodman, "Do the Poor Pay More?", *Journal of Marketing*, Vol. 32, No. 1 (January 1968).

U. S. Department of Labor, Bureau of Labor Statistics, "A Study of Prices Charged in Food Stores Located in Low and Higher Income Areas of Six Large Cities, February, 1966" (Washington: U. S. Government Printing Office, 1966).

Federal Trade Commission, *Economic Report on Food Chain Selling Practices in the District of Columbia and San Francisco*, (Washington: U. S. Government Printing Office, 1969).

Donald E. Sexton, Jr., *Do Blacks Pay More?* (unpublished doctoral dissertation, University of Chicago, 1970).

economy, however; they permit the poor to buy major durable goods that normal channels of trade do not provide. The poor pay more, but they obtain goods that they would otherwise be unable to buy.

Caplovitz points out that one reason for the high prices and credit costs of ghetto retailing is the higher risks associated with selling to the poor. These risks cause businessmen in other retail areas to turn down such customers. Ghetto business establishments respond to this gap in the market by devising the business practices that enable them to sell to the poor and still make a profit.[2]

A second feature of ghetto retailing is the fact that a very large portion of the customers are black. This has led to a racially segregated market in some areas of retailing which has enabled black business enterprise to develop. In part the segregated market exists because of geographical considerations. Some types of retail stores stick close to a neighborhood simply because people do not want to travel far to buy food, personal care products, and similar items. At the same time, business capital requirements and the size of the market make possible dispersal of many small retail units of neighborhood size.

Another reason for the segregated market is the historical unwillingness of enterprises catering to whites to serve blacks. Until World War II this included many substantial retail outlets such as department and furniture stores and, until very recently, restaurants, hotels, and similar establishments. For example, in a segregated city like Washington, D. C., before the 1950s blacks who shopped in the downtown retail district could expect rude treatment, designed to discourage their patronage, while inability to use eating places (and rest rooms) made shopping difficult.[3]

Closely related pressures from the white community restricted the practice of most black lawyers, doctors, dentists, accountants, and other professionals to the urban ghetto and black clientele. Certain types of personal services such as hair cutting and cosmetics have become black business specialties because of the special needs and fashions of black customers.

---

[2]On the problems of business enterprises in the inner city, see National Conference on Small Business, *Problems and Opportunities Confronting Negroes in the Field of Business* (Washington: U. S. Government Printing Office, 1962); President's National Advisory Panel on Insurance in Riot-Affected Areas, *Hearings* (Washington: U. S. Government Printing Office, 1968), and *Meeting the Insurance Crisis of Our Cities* (Washington: U. S. Government Printing Office, 1968).

[3]Constance M. Green, *The Secret City: A History of Race Relations in the Nation's Capital* (Princeton: Princeton University Press, 1967), pp. 3, 298.

Black Business Enterprise

Black-owned business enterprise reflects the quasi-segregated nature of the ghetto market. Firms are centered in personal services and retail trade, with a scattering of other services and construction. Although very little precise information is available, the U. S. Small Business Administration estimated that some 158,000 business enterprises were owned in 1969 by nonwhites, out of a national total of some 5,420,000, or 2.9 percent.[4] The great bulk of the nonwhite owners were, of course, black people. The nonwhite-owned businesses were distributed among industries as shown in Table 7.1.

TABLE 7.1

Nonwhite-owned Business Enterprises, 1969

INDUSTRY	NUMBER OF FIRMS (000)	PERCENT OF NONWHITE BUSINESS ENTERPRISES
Retail trade	71.0	45.0
Personal services	33.0	20.9
Other services	20.7	13.1
Construction	8.1	5.1
Wholesale trade	5.8	3.7
Manufacturing	2.6	1.6
Other	16.8	10.6
Total	158.0	100.0

SOURCE: U. S. Department of Commerce, Small Business Administration, *Quarterly Economic Digest 2* (Winter), 1969, p. 26.

Most black-owned business enterprises are found in central city areas, and especially in urban poverty areas, in contrast to white-owned businesses, which are not located in slum areas to any significant extent. The contrast in location is shown in Table 7.2. Although heavily concentrated in central city areas and in slums, they do not comprise a majority of the business enterprises there, even in the urban ghettos. In New York's Harlem a study of street-level businesses showed that only some 53 percent were owned by

[4]U. S. Department of Commerce, Small Business Administration, *Quarterly Economic Digest 2* (Winter 1969), pp. 26-27.

blacks. Studies of similar areas in other cities show nonwhite ownership varying from 20 to 40 percent. The Small Business Administration estimated in 1969 that in central city ghettos in the nation as a
whole nonwhites owned only 26 percent of the business establishments.

TABLE 7.2

**Location of Black-owned and White-owned
Business Enterprises, 1969**
(percent)

LOCATION	BLACK-OWNED[a]		WHITE-OWNED	
Urban, 50,000 and over	71.9		45.6	
Slum		33.3		3.4
Other central city		35.1		30.3
Suburban		3.5		11.9
Urban, under 50,000 and rural	28.1		54.4	
Total	100.0		100.0	

SOURCE: U. S. Small Business Administration, *Fact Sheet* (Washington:
May 19, 1969, mimeo).
[a]Does not include firms owned by other nonwhite minorities.

Black-owned enterprises are small operations, often run by an
individual or a small family, and have few employees. In most size
dimensions they are smaller than white-owned enterprises. Some
relevant comparisons are shown in Table 7.3.

Although primarily engaged in small retail trade, food services,
and personal services, black business has developed a rudimentary
network of manufacturing and wholesale trade to back up the retail
and service enterprises. For example, black entrepreneurs manufacture cosmetics for black-owned beauty parlors, and some of the
distribution is done by black-owned wholesale outlets. Since the
black markets are relatively small, the supporting production and
distribution network is also relatively small.

There is also an infrastructure of black-owned newspapers,
banks, and insurance companies. This sector is relatively small but
highly significant for black business and the black community. In
1967 there were seventeen black-owned banks (out of a national

TABLE 7.3

Size Comparisons, White-owned and Minority-owned Business Enterprises

NUMBER OF PAID EMPLOYEES	MINORITY-OWNED (PERCENT)	OTHER (PERCENT)
0	32.5	26.0
1-9	61.0	55.0
10-49	5.0	13.2
50-99	1.2	2.7
100 and over	—	3.1
Gross receipts ($000)		
0-9.9	33.4	18.7
10-19.9	14.8	12.5
20-49.9	18.5	19.4
50-99.9	11.1	14.7
100-999.9	19.8	25.8
1,000-4,999.9	1.2	6.2
5000 and over	1.2	2.7

SOURCE: U. S. Small Business Administration, *Fact Sheet* (Washington: May 19, 1969, mimeo).

total of some 12,000) with total assets of about $147 millions (0.039 percent of the national total). These banks were small, weak, and not highly profitable, although their growth record has been comparatively good in recent years.[5] Life insurance companies owned by blacks have a similar record: they are growing well, but have a very small share of the market. Twenty companies in 1962, which held almost all the assets of some fifty black-owned insurance companies, had 0.75 percent of industry sales while holding only about 0.25 percent of industry assets. This reflects both the growing demand for insurance by blacks and the tendency of smaller insurance companies to grow faster than the industry average. Nevertheless, their proportion of the business is very small. In general, black-owned companies tend to follow conservative investment policies and have lagged

[5]Andrew F. Brimmer, "The Banking System and Urban Economic Development," Address delivered to the joint session of the 1968 Annual Meetings of the American Real Estate and Urban Economics Association and the American Finance Association, Chicago, December 28, 1968 (mimeo).

in entering some of the newer areas of the industry.[6] In the last few years a number of black-owned banks and several insurance companies have been formed. The larger number is important for the black community, but they are relatively small and have not as yet had much impact.

The Segregated Market

The segregated nature of the market for the products and services of black business enterprise, together with its small size and concentration in retail and service industry, create significant problems of economic development. Three conflicting trends can be observed.

The long-term trend until the mid-1960s was one of relative decline. Black enterprise appeared as a decreasingly significant factor in the national economy, even within urban ghetto areas. Several developments lay behind this trend:

1. While growing in numbers, small business enterprise in general has been declining in relative importance. This is particularly true of retail trade, where large chain store distribution has become the dominant pattern.

2. Urban renewal and low-cost housing projects have taken a heavy toll of the small enterprises located in urban ghetto areas.

3. As black incomes have risen, a growing proportion of black spending has gone into "big ticket" items, such as automobiles, household appliances, furniture, and related purchases. These sectors of the retail market are not segregated and are served almost exclusively by white-owned enterprises.

4. As the urban black population has increased and the size of the black market has grown, it has been penetrated by white-owned enterprise taking advantage of larger opportunities for profits.

The situation is indeed paradoxical. A once highly segregated market grows in both numbers of customers and in average income. The result is not a corresponding growth of the black business to serve this market, but a penetration of white enterprise. At the same

[6]Andrew F. Brimmer, "The Negro in the American Economy," in John P. Davis (ed.), *The American Negro Reference Book* (Englewood Cliffs, N. J.: Prentice-Hall, 1966), pp. 251-336.

time the segregation of the black market tends to break down as blacks begin to use the ordinary white channels of trade to a greater extent.

The second trend has been more recent. Following the uprisings of 1966 and 1967, white-owned business enterprises have tended to move out of ghetto areas or, if destroyed, to remain closed. This has opened the way for black entrepreneurs to replace them. How extensive this shift has been is a matter of conjecture, for substantiating data is lacking and the evidence is largely that of casual observation. The source of the shift has been dual. On the one hand, whites have moved out of ghetto businesses in large part as a result of uncertainty and fear. On the other hand, a growing awareness of black business by ghetto residents themselves—both a cause and a result of the uprisings—has stimulated black buying from black businessmen. This shift in consumer and community attitudes in the urban ghettos stimulated the movement to promote black business enterprise, community economic development, and the expansion of Black banks and other financial institutions.

Finally, the spread of urban blight in the inner city cores of many metropolitan areas has brought boarded-up storefronts, bankruptcies, and general decline of commercial activity. Few of the burned-out areas of major cities have been rebuilt. Some of the old shopping areas, like 125th Street in Harlem, are flourishing, but the more typical pattern is one of decay.[7]

It is too early to tell whether these developments will have a significant impact on the ghetto economy. The fact remains that most ghetto residents spend their incomes with business enterprises whose capital comes from outside the ghetto, whose ownership is outside the ghetto, whose sales and administrative personnel live outside the ghetto, and which sell products produced outside the ghetto. The flow of purchases, wage payments, profits, and other expenditures sets up a flow from the ghetto to the larger economy outside. By contrast, the circular flow of spending within the ghetto, which goes from customer to enterprise to employment and payments back to customer, is meager. It is limited to a narrow and fragile segment of small retail and service enterprises, which, until very recently, was declining in importance rather than growing.

---

[7]"Inner City Decay Causes Life to Wither," *New York Times*, July 19, 1971, pp. 1, 29.

Black Capitalism

A huge amount of publicity has been given to "black capitalism."[8] During the 1968 presidential campaign Richard Nixon advocated programs that would enlist private funds, talent, and organizations in programs to develop opportunities for black business enterprise, with the support of the federal government. Black business leadership was to be developed that would provide leadership to the black community and offer an example to others. The image was one of individual success within a capitalist system in which opportunities were open to those who take them—a sort of Horatio Alger strive-and-succeed program under the guidance of successful white enterprise.

The rhetoric of black capitalism is based in large part on a mythology that ceased long ago to have much relevance. The path to business success today, even for white Protestants, is largely by climbing the ladders of the business hierarchies already established in large corporations, and not by trying to build a new enterprise in industries already dominated by oligopolistic giants. In those sectors of the economy in which competitive small business flourishes competition is strong and newcomers must face rivalry with established businessmen wise in the ways of survival in a ruthless world. Those conditions are particularly strong in the business world of the inner city. Any program of black capitalism designed to appeal to blacks who desire business success must overcome two great obstacles. Intelligent, business-oriented young blacks will try to move into the management training and selection procedures of large firms, just as their white counterparts do. Others, who take the path of developing their own enterprises, will have a high rate of failure, just like their white counterparts, and relatively few will succeed.

Another factor operates against black capitalism. One element in the developing ideology of inner city ghettos is a feeling of group solidarity among minority groups. The individualism of black capital-

[8]Books and articles on black capitalism run the gamut from laudatory advocacy to condemnation. A characteristic favorable presentation, written by a white lawyer, is Theodore L. Cross, *Black Capitalism: Strategy for Business in the Ghetto* (New York: Atheneum, 1969). Counterarguments from a radical perspective are made in Earl Ofari, *The Myth of Black Capitalism* (New York: Monthly Review Press, 1970). Other useful articles and books are Robert B. McKersie, "Vitalize Black Enterprise," *Harvard Business Review* (Sept.-Oct. 1968), pp. 88-99; Frederick D. Sturdivant, "The Limits of Black Capitalism," *Harvard Business Review* (Jan.-Feb. 1969), pp. 122-128; The American Assembly, *Black Economic Development* (New York: Arden House, 1969); Eugene P. Foley, *The Achieving Ghetto* (Washington: National Press, 1968); and Ronald W. Bailey (ed.), *Black Business Enterprise* (New York: Basic Books, 1971).

ism does not satisfy the feeling that the community as a whole must move to greater affluence and control over its own destiny, and not just individuals within it. Black capitalism was poorly conceived not only economically, but also psychologically.

Whatever the faults in conception may have been, the deficiencies in execution were worse. The Small Business Administration (SBA), whose record of aid to minority-owned enterprises had been dismal, began in late 1968 to increase substantially the amount and proportions of its loans to nonwhite enterprises. This program became a victim of both tight fiscal policies and the inherent flaws in the concept. Little money was available in an administration that held back federal spending in a futile effort to stop an inflation it did not start and could not halt. And the loss rate on loans to nonwhite businesses turned out to be four times as high as loss rates on loans to white-owned firms. As a result of these factors, and probably because of political considerations as well (the black communities never strongly embraced the idea of black capitalism), the SBA's loan program fell far below its targets and by 1970 was stabilized at a low level. At best a token, its impact has been negligible and has failed completely to effect any significant changes in the economy of the inner city ghettos.

Other federal programs to aid black business enterprise have had similar histories. Small, scattered, and uncoordinated, ineffectual and poorly financed, they provide a Potemkin-village facade that hides the reality of unconcern and lack of commitment. No significant federal effort has been made to assist substantially black business enterprise. However, the federal government has provided guarantees of loans of $100 million to the Penn Central Railroad and $250 million to Lockheed Aircraft Corporation.

Big Business in the Ghetto

Business investment in ghetto enterprises in the inner city has also failed to develop adequately. This was the conclusion reached by a report released in May 1971 by the Conference Board, a business-sponsored research organization, which surveyed 30 subsidiaries or affiliates of large corporations established from 1966 to 1970 in 15 central city areas.[9]

[9]*Business and the Development of Ghetto Enterprise* (New York: The Conference Board, 1971). For comment on the report, see "Reaction Mixed in Ghetto Study," *New York Times*, May 31, 1971.

Most of the enterprises encountered serious problems. Costs were high. Excessively ambitious goals were the general rule, resulting in cutbacks and disillusionment among employees and the community. Unfamiliar products and processes resulted in delays and failure to meet production targets. In addition to these difficulties associated with new businesses, the general business recession of 1969-1970 brought reduced sales, the federal government cut back spending for defense and aerospace, and established firms (including parent companies) failed to become strong customers. One important cause of their problems was the failure of private enterprise and government to support the enterprises by commiting funds to purchase their output in amounts that would assure success. When the government did place an order with the ghetto firms, there were long delays in negotiating contracts.

The Conference Board concluded that most of the enterprises did not meet "the conventional business criteria of productive efficiency and profit," although some were successful by those standards.

Watts Manufacturing Corporation was the first inner city ghetto enterprise established by outside business firms to try to meet the employment needs of the ghetto. It was started in 1966 adjacent to the Watts district of Los Angeles, scene of the first of the major inner city riots in 1964, and was formed by a group of blacks and by Aerojet General Corporation, a subsidiary of General Tire and Rubber Company. The enterprise obtained contracts to produce for both its parent and the federal government, and employment rose quickly to about 500 persons. It ran into serious difficulties, however. An ambitious training program set up for unskilled workers proved to be a high-cost operation. Too many workers were hired, and initially the work force had high rates of turnover and absenteeism. These difficulties forced large reductions in the scope of the operation. By mid-1970 the enterprise was stabilized with about 200 employees and could be classified as a limited success.

The lack of success of most of the projects was not due to some factors that their originators had feared. Residents of the ghettos sought jobs in the new enterprises and were reliable workers. The community looked with favor upon the establishment of firms controlled by outside capital. White managers were accepted by workers. In these respects the inner city ghettos responded much like any community selected by a large firm for establishment of a new plant.

Yet in spite of the know-how and business expertise of established parent companies that these inner city enterprises could draw upon, in spite of the presence of an available and willing labor supply, and in spite of general community acceptance, the bulk of these enterprises have floundered. Most have survived, but they have not prospered.

In retrospect, the greatest deficiency seems to have been lack of adequate markets. Even highly inefficient enterprises can become moderate successes if customers take their products, and whether these inner city establishments are any more inefficient than some giant firms (compare them with Lockheed, Penn Central, or American Telephone and Telegraph) is at least arguable. The lack of markets can be attributed directly to policies of the federal government: the aggregative economic policies that brought on the 1969-1970 recession and the failure of federal procurement agencies to allocate adequate funds for purchases from inner city and minority-owned enterprises. If federal policy to promote private enterprise in the ghetto is to be successful, a general economic environment of prosperity is necessary, along with specific commitment of substantial federal purchases. Up to this point, neither of these conditions have prevailed.

Community Development Corporations

The inner city has not been able to rely upon either black capitalism or the private efforts of large coporations to stimulate economic development. The limitations and failures of those approaches, together with the rise of black nationalism and growing feelings of community solidarity, brought to the fore a movement to promote community development corporations. This movement began in the mid-1960s as a response of the black community itself to its own problem of economic development. Most major cities now have one or more projects involving the community as a whole. Federal legislation to promote them was proposed in 1968 but was not passed.[10]

[10]There is not much literature on inner city community economic development activities. Some information on the concepts involved can be obtained from Richard S. Rosenbloom, "Corporations for Urban Development," in Rosenbloom and Robin Marris, *Social Innovation in the City: New Enterprises for Community Development* (Cambridge: Harvard University Program on Technology and Society, 1969); and Bennett Harrison, "A Pilot Project in Economic Development Planning for American Urban Slums," *International Development Review* Vol. X, No. 1 (March 1968), pp. 23-29. The proposed federal legislation was Senate Bill 3876, 90th Congress, 2nd Session; see U. S. Senate, *Hearings, Community Self-Determination Act* (Washington: U. S. Government Printing

The Inner City Business Improvement Forum (ICBIF) in Detroit is a typical example. It has a board of directors drawn from the minority inner city population. Its objective is improvement of the economic base of the inner city and widened economic opportunity for its residents. Any project supported by ICBIF must have some form of community involvement—community or employee ownership, cooperative enterprise, or some type of profit sharing that feeds capital back into the inner city. Since its formation in the mid-1960s the Detroit project has sponsored establishment of a black-owned inner city bank, a cooperative retail enterprise, and a housing rehabilitation and construction firm. The first two were successful, but the third failed. It also supports the establishment of privately owned firms that will employ workers in the inner city. Assisting ICBIF is a white Economic Development Corporation whose primary function is to channel business expertise and capital from white firms into inner city enterprises. One chief function of ICBIF is to act as liaison between local development projects and federal programs, assisting in developing projects and grant applications for the projects it helps sponsor.

Two fundamental points characterize ICBIF and the other community economic development organizations. First, they are oriented toward improvement of the entire community. Individual gain is important, but secondary. Some form of "community dividend" is envisaged, along with a coordinated plan of development. Second, community development corporations act as a channel by which capital, expert knowledge, and federal assistance are channeled into the inner city ghetto. In this respect they offer hope for reversing the usual drain of resources and human capital out of the ghetto. Most of the plans, however, are simple and rudimentary at the present time because of the small scale of most of the operations.

Community development corporations are not a large element in the ghetto economy. Federal legislation that would have promoted their growth was not passed. Yet the beginnings made by them in most inner city areas represent a promising start. They provide an alternative strategy to the individualistic and private efforts that have gained the bulk of support from outside the inner city but which have been ineffective and limited in their results.

Office, 1968). This legislation is attacked in Sturdivant, *op. cit.*, pp. 122-128. A strong case for community development corporations is made in Twentieth Century Fund, *CDCs: New Hope for the Inner City* (New York: Twentieth Century Fund, 1971).

Barriers to Economic Development of the Inner City

The inner city does not provide a favorable environment for the development of economic activity. The internal market is weak. Poor people make poor customers and do not generate large amounts of resources for economic growth.

The inner city lacks capital, and a persistent drain of resources from the ghetto prevents it from accumulating significant amounts of capital. Both public agencies and private sources have been unable or unwilling to generate more than token flows of capital inward to the inner city. The lack of capital is the most important barrier to the economic development of the inner city: markets could be found outside, especially through government contracts, but capital must be found to provide resources for production.

The twin barriers of inadequate capital and poor markets could be overcome by economic development and assistance plans analogous to those applied in some of the developing countries abroad. One proposal was the "Ghetto Economic Development and Industrialization Plan" prepared by Dunbar S. McLaurin for the Human Resources Administration of New York City.[11] Funds would be provided through inner city banks, which would receive deposits of city funds on condition that they make development loans to ten development corporations in the ghetto areas. Five of the corporations would be local development corporations that would try to attract or develop new enterprises in the inner city. The other five corporations would be Small Business Investment Companies that would provide loans and venture capital to private enterprises. Included in the planning is a guaranteed market for the inner city enterprises provided by purchases by the city government. Ultimately, all of the enterprises and development corporations would be sold to stockholders in the inner city. The strategy of McLaurin's GHEDIplan was simple: enterprises involving people in the ghettos would be provided with outside capital to produce primarily for guaranteed outside markets. Nothing has come of the GHEDIplan, however. Implementation was not feasible, and it has been placed on the shelf.

Two other proposals for ghetto economic development are based

[11]Dunbar S. McLaurin, "GHEDIPLAN, An Economic Development Plan Prepared for the Human Resources Administration of the City of New York," (New York: Human Resources Administration, April 1968). The plan is discussed in Dunbar S. McLaurin and Cyril D. Tyson, "The GHEDIPLAN for Economic Development," in William F. Haddad and G. Douglas Pugh (eds.), *Black Economic Development* (Englewood Cliffs, N.J.: Prentice-Hall, 1969), pp. 126-137.

on the concept of community ownership and participation. Vietorisz and Harrison propose a scheme for the development of Harlem-based "greenhouse industries." These would be community-owned enterprises whose chief function would be to upgrade the work skills of their employees prior to placing them in outside jobs. The authors also advocate community-owned stores and other facilities to serve the community. A program of even larger scope is suggested by Frank G. Davis, who proposes a federally owned National Ghetto Development Corporation to nationalize all ghetto business enterprises, sell them to local community enterprises, and assist in their expansion. These enterprises would be supplemented by National Ghetto Investment Banks and Credit Corporations designed to reverse the outward flow of resources and bring capital into the ghettos. Davis would also seek to promote ghetto economic growth by diverting some of the earnings of ghetto labor into capital accumulation.[12]

The most important barriers to inner city development programs do not appear to be economic, but political. Decisions about the use of public resources are made by the great majority of middle-income whites who live outside the inner city ghettos. Their interests are not served by changing present conditions, but by preserving them. As long as that situation prevails, even programs oriented strongly toward private enterprise, like McLaurin's GHEDIplan, cannot get started.

Development of inner city business enterprise offers little hope for solutions to the economic problems of the ghetto. Black capitalism might, at best, create a small business elite, but it does not provide a means of advancement for the great majority. As long as it serves the limited ghetto market, its prospects are themselves limited, and gaining markets outside the ghetto is difficult at best. Location of satellite plants in the ghetto has had only very limited success; that has also been true of community development corporations. Economic development programs like the GHEDIplan have been unable to overcome political barriers to capital and markets. With an inadequate internal market and difficulty in producing for outside markets, ghetto business enterprise and economic development are severely limited.

[12]Thomas Vietorisz and Bennett Harrison, *The Economic Development of Harlem* (New York: Praeger, 1970), and "Ghetto Development, Community Corporations and Public Policy," *Review of Black Political Economy*, Vol. 2, No. 1 (Fall 1971), pp. 28-73; Frank G. Davis, *The Economics of Black Community Development: An Analysis and Program for Autonomous Growth and Development* (Chicago: Markham, 1972).

CHAPTER 8

Can We Solve the Problem?

This book has shown that the urban racial problem is deeply rooted in the economic structure of the United States. The problem is one of exploitation of racial minorities from which the white majority benefits in specific, material ways. This economic exploitation is strengthened and solidified by racial attitudes that indentify the exploited minority, justify its exploitation, and provide a psychological rationale for those who benefit. Whether white racism is the cause of economic exploitation, the result of it, or both is immaterial. The fundamental problem is economic.

The problem is complicated by the fact that individual acts of exploitation or overt discrimination are seldom necessary. The whole structure of the economic system crowds minorities into low-wage menial occupations and segregates them in urban ghettos. The ghetto then becomes a source of low-wage labor; it is directly exploited by outside economic interests; and it provides a dumping ground for the human residuals created by economic change. These economic conditions are stabilized by transfer payments that preserve the ghetto in a poverty that recreates itself from generation to generation.

Any solutions will have to break up the economic relationships on which exploitation is based. An underclass of low-wage workers will have to be admitted to the relative affluence of the rest of the society. The high rates of unemployment that preserve the low-wage system will have to be eliminated. These two propositions, full employment at a living wage, entail a substantial redistribution of income. If the bottom 20 percent of American families are to obtain a larger share of the good things in life, the upper 80 percent will have to share a smaller proportion of our affluence. This is the hard decision we will have to make: strategies that ignore this fundamental proposition are destined to fail.

Two Ineffective Strategies

Discussion of solutions of the urban racial problem has been dominated by two strategies. Both are in the liberal reformist tradition in that they do not imply significant changes in the structure of power or the distribution of income and wealth. One is the strategy of integration, which would disperse the present ghettos and spread their populations broadly through urban areas. The other is the strategy of improvement, which would provide money and public services to improve the quality of ghetto life.

Dispersal of blacks and other minority groups into nonghetto parts of metropolitan areas is not the answer.[1] Even if it were accompanied by improved housing, education, and other public services and even if it brought improved access to suburban industrial jobs, a geographical shift of racial minorities and the poor to the suburbs, would disperse the economic conditions of the ghetto into relatively small pockets of poverty (minighettos) throughout suburban areas. It would also disperse whatever political influence the geographically concentrated ghettos now have, thereby making effective solutions to the economic problem more difficult to achieve. It is not the intent of those liberals who advocate solutions based on racial integration to diminish the political influence of the ghetto, but that is exactly what ghetto dispersal would do. It is a program that would maintain the economic status quo while changing housing relationships between the races.

The strategy of dispersal is based on the assumption that racial attitudes are at the root of the problem. It aims at breaking down antagonisms through familiarity and social contact. But without a direct attack on the economic roots of exploitation of minority groups it will leave the present economic conflicts untouched. If those economic conflicts are the underpinning of racism, little progress can be expected.

Policies that would "gild the ghetto" are equally open to criticism. Subsidies for housing, medical care programs, improved educational facilities, and urban transportation and larger welfare payments could make ghetto life more bearable. These types of programs can raise both the real and money incomes of ghetto residents, and thereby improve their economic condition. But when seen as part of the larger economic relationships between the ghetto and the economy outside the ghetto, two considerations indicate why those measures do not solve the problem.

First, transfers of real and money income to the ghetto come from taxpayers outside the ghetto who have a general interest in preserv-

[1]The case for dispersal of the ghetto is most forcefully presented in John F. Kain and Joseph Persky, "Alternatives to the Gilded Ghetto," *The Public Interest*, No. 14 (Winter 1969). For a critique of the Kain–Persky view, see Peter Labrie, "Black Central Cities: Dispersal or Rebuilding," *Review of Black Political Economy*, Vol. 1, No. 2 (Autumn 1970), pp. 3-27 and Vol. I, No. 3, pp. 78-99.

ing the existence of a low-wage sector. They can hardly be expected to maintain transfers at a level higher than the minimum necessary to preserve social and economic stability. This political reality condemns income transfers and subsidies to levels too low to bring fundamental changes.

Second, the persistent flow of income and resources out of the ghetto would continue. Larger incomes for the ghetto pouulation mean an enlarged flow through the ghetto. The chief beneficiaries would not be ghetto residents, but those in strategic positions to benefit from the flow through of income and resources. These beneficiaries are numerous: absentee landlords, managers and workers in the criminal industries, middle-income employees of the welfare bureaucracies and school systems, developers of low-income housing projects and the union members employed in the construction industries, and similarly situated people. One effect of a higher level of ghetto life sustained by income transfers and more public services will be an enlarged group that benefits from the drain of income and has a vested interest in continuing things as they are. The strategy of improvement will strengthen the economic position of those who live off the ghetto without removing the causes of ghettoization.

A Nonrevolutionary Program for Revolutionary Change

Serious proposals for eliminating the urban ghetto must involve changes in the economic relationships that sustain the ghetto economy and preserve the low-wage labor force, which is its chief economic feature. Such changes imply elimination of the poverty-ridden underclass that largely makes up that labor force. That can be done only if there is a significant shift in the distribution of income from the relatively affluent to the poor—not through transfer payments, but through the normal functioning of the economy. Put bluntly, *the poor must earn a living wage if the urban ghetto is to be eliminated and America's economic underclass is to participate effectively in whatever economic progress is made*. This is the revolutionary change that must be the keystone of any real solution of the urban racial problem.

The means for achieving these changes are available. A group of programs and policies that build upon ones that have already been tried and everyone is familiar with can be used. They attack the economic basis of the ghetto economy by concentrating on the employment problems and low-wage occupations that create its permanent depression and poverty.

Full Employment

The first requisite is full employment. A job for anyone wishing to work is necessary if the permanent depression of the ghetto economy is to be eliminated. Simply increasing aggregate demand by fiscal and monetary policies is not enough, for inflationary conditions will appear in the larger economy before the ghetto approaches full employment. Increases in aggregate demand will have to be supplemented by special employment programs that reach the ghetto unemployed. One possible approach could be the following:

1. Monetary and fiscal policies can be used to bring unemployment rates for white men aged 25 to 44 down to the pure "frictional" unemployment rate of 1 to 1.5 percent.
2. At that point ghetto unemployment rates may still be as high as 6 to 7 percent. Special employment programs aimed at ghetto residents can then be used to bring ghetto unemployment rates down to levels prevailing in the rest of the economy.

A wide variety of employment programs could be used for this purpose. Public service employment, youth employment programs, or programs to encourage private employment of ghetto residents could be developed. The important point is that jobs should be made available by a combination of general prosperity and special employment programs focusing on the ghetto.

The only revolutionary aspect of these proposals for job creation is their magnitude. It may be necessary to provide jobs for as many as 5 million persons, particularly if minimum wage rates are raised to levels that provide adequate support for a family. An employment program of that scope could be expensive. Suppose, for example, we were to employ 5 million persons at full-time jobs in public service employment at $3.50 per hour. The annual cost would be $35 billion. That total could be reduced by providing tax and other incentives to business enterprises for hiring some of the 5 million. And reduced costs for welfare and other social services to the poor, and for police protection, might chop off a significant part of the total. Nevertheless, the potential annual cost of full employment for the ghettos might be as high as $35 billion.

A Living Wage

The second requisite for fundamental change in the economics of the ghetto is the most important; employment at a living wage. According to 1971 estimates made by the Bureau of Labor Statistics of the Department of Labor, a minimum health and decency income for an urban family of four would equal almost $7,000 annually. That is equivalent to an hourly wage of $3.50 for a fully employed person, based on a 40-hour work week for 50 weeks 9 the year.

$$
\begin{array}{r}
40 \text{ hours employment per week} \\
\underline{\times\ 50 \text{ weeks per year}} \\
2{,}000 \text{ hours of work per year} \\
\underline{\times\ \$3.50 \text{ per hour}} \\
\$7{,}000 \text{ annual income}
\end{array}
$$

Therefore, $3.50 per hour, at present, should be the standard for a revised and extended minimum wage law. The minimum wage should be set at the level that provides a minimum health and decency income for an urban family of four when one member of the family is employed full time. Coverage should be extended to all workers. If consumer prices rose, the minimum would be adjusted upward. It might also be adjusted downward if prices fell, but that might be hard to accomplish (and price levels have not fallen significantly at any time in the last quarter century, making the question somewhat academic).

This is perhaps the most controversial part of the proposal set forth here, and the one most difficult for many to accept. It has tremendous implications for the entire economy. Before it is rejected out of hand, note this: Australian minimum wage legislation is written exactly the way that we propose here; whatever may be the problems of the Australian economy, few experts attribute them to minimum wage legislation. A minimum health and decency wage is the fastest and best way to end the poverty and depressed conditions of the ghetto, with the proviso that it must be accompanied by a full-employment program of the sort just described if it is to increase ghetto incomes properly.

With higher incomes many of the other problems of the ghetto will be greatly reduced, and some may disappear entirely. Higher incomes will enable many of the poor to provide for their own transportation, either by public transportation or private cars. Cities may have to adjust by providing more extensive public transportation systems and more effective patterns of traffic control. But their revenue potential will also be increased because of higher incomes earned by their citizens. Higher incomes will enable ghettoites to move out of the ghettos if they wish, (and if housing segregation is prevented) since they will be able to afford housing in other areas. Within the ghettos effective demand for better housing will trigger a response from the housing industry. Strongly responsive to market demand, the industry can be expected to respond relatively quickly by providing the better housing that buyers or renters could now afford. Many public services, including education, could be expanded and improved because of the higher revenues cities would obtain from their higher income citizens, for prosperous people create prosperous communities.

Business enterprise within the ghetto would be stimulated by the increase in purchasing power. With higher family incomes and greater financial stability one could confidently predict a relative decline in the exploitive ghetto business community that stresses high prices and easy credit. A better climate for less exploitive business-consumer relationships would also result. The basis for ghetto-owned private, cooperative, or community business enterprises would be improved. Indeed, one could predict both a partial breakdown of the barriers between the ghetto and the rest of the economy and a stronger basis for economic development within the ghetto.

Training and Retraining

One obvious disadvantage of an hourly minimum wage of $3.50 is its impact on employment. Economic analysis of the effect of minimum wage legislation on levels of employment is not conclusive, largely because it is difficult to assess the relative importance of the short-run effects (increased business costs) against the long-run effects (higher purchasing power). Nevertheless, it may be necessary to maintain large special employment programs for low-wage workers to compensate for the unemployment created by a higher minimum wage. Earlier in this chapter the possible cost of such a program for as many as 5 million workers was estimated at $35 billion annually.

These considerations lead to some modifications of the minimum wage proposal. First, the minimum wage could be increased by stages over a three-to four-year period in order to provide more time for both business firms and workers to prepare for and adjust to it. A step-by-step increase of 50 cents a year for three years, or 75 cents a year for two years, may be the best way to introduce such a large change, instead of moving up by the full amount in one leap.

Second, a substantially expanded program of training and education for low-skilled workers will undoubtedly be needed. The costs of such a program might well be large when compared with the relatively small amounts now spent for those purposes. But in terms of total Federal expenditures and revenues the costs would be well within reason.

Suppose that raising the minimum wage to $3.50 per hour were to cause employers to lay off 8 million workers over a three-year period in which the minimum wage is raised by steps to the new level. That number represents one-tenth of the labor force and is probably an excessively large number if past studies of the effects of increases in the minimum wage can be relied upon. Nevertheless, how much would it cost to upgrade 8 million workers to reach the higher levels of productivity that would enable them to keep jobs that paid $3.50 per hour, either in private or public service employment? We can use an outside estimate of perhaps $2,000 per worker, based on the costs in the present manpower development and training program. That would make the total cost equal to $16 billion. The total cost equals the cost of about 6 months of the Vietnam war at the peak of war expenditures. Spread over a three-year period, it would equal a little more than $5 billion annually. Even if the employment effects of the increased minimum wage were double those estimated here, the cost of retraining for the affected workers would be readily manageable.

The costs of retraining and placement are small compared to the costs of public service employment. To the extent that the former can substitute for the latter, the costs of a program for full employment at a living wage can be greatly reduced. But training and placement services will not overcome all of the unemployment effects of a large and rapid increase in the minimum wage. A large public service employment program will be needed.

A Guaranteed Income

Not every family has a wage earner. The aged, the disabled, and broken families require financial assistance. They are not reached by minimum wage legislation and would have to be helped, as they now are, by transfer payments. As Chapter 6 pointed out, however, the present level of transfer payments is seriously inadequate. Support levels in the welfare system, for example, provide assistance at about half the amount necessary for minimum subsistence, about half of those in need obtain assistance, and current proposals would not do much better.

If workers are able to earn a living wage, it becomes possible to set standards for transfer payments at decent levels without interfering significantly with work incentives. The minimum subsistence level immediately suggests itself as a reasonable standard. For a family of four in 1972, that would equal about $4,800 annually (using the Bureau of Labor Statistics estimates) or about $4,000 (using the admittedly low Welfare Administration estimates). All income transfer programs, including welfare payments, aid to the disabled, and social security benefits should be keyed to that level as a minimum.

It could be argued that a guaranteed income at the subsistence level encourages laziness and would create a permanently idle portion of the work force that is unwilling to work. There may indeed be such an effect, but we should not expect it to be large. Most Americans, whatever their racial or cultural background, are motivated by a desire to live well and to succeed as income earners. Not all are able to do so. Some become discouraged by repeated failures and rebuffs and effectively lose all or part of the desire to better themselves. But these economic failures are the result, in part, of an economic system that has a high incidence of unemployment and pays low wages in dead-end jobs for many workers. Discouragement is built into the system. An economy that sustains full employment and pays a living wage to everyone willing to work will be less frustrating and more encouraging. In such an economy a subsistence income will hardly beckon many people, when so much more can be gained by work.[2]

At the present time, when a full-time, low-wage worker may not earn enough to maintain a family of four above the poverty line, welfare and other transfer payments are kept low in order not to damage the incentive to work. The result is the worst type of poverty

[2] Idleness among the poor is deplored, but idleness among the wealthy is celebrated. We hear much criticism of transfer payments to the poor, even though present levels are below subsistence. Yet there is little opposition to unearned income for the rich who wile away their time at Palm Beach or Acapulco; those incomes are just as much a drain on the economy as are transfer payments to the poor. If idleness among the poor is deplorable, why is not idleness among the rich?

for those receiving public assistance. Once wage rates are raised to enable a full-time worker to earn enough to maintain a family in full health and decency, it will be possible to raise levels of public assistance at least to the poverty line.

A Digression: Broader Economic Policies and the Problem of Inflation

One of the common objections to proposals that would significantly increase the minimum wage is that such action would be inflationary. Costs of production in the low-wage industries would rise, causing upward pressure on prices. If federal fiscal and monetary policies maintain aggregate demand at full-employment levels, the cost pressures could easily lead to price increases. The price increases would not only cancel out a large portion of the benefits from the higher minimum wage, but they could also trigger demands for wage increases by other workers that, in turn, would push up prices in other sectors of the economy as well. An inflationary spiral might be established that would push up prices to significantly higher levels.

There is some validity in this argument. At the very least, prices in the low-wage industries would undoubtedly be adjusted upward to compensate at least partly for the higher costs imposed by an increase in the minimum wage of the amounts proposed here. Whether an inflationary spiral would be established is another matter, for much depends upon the measures taken to avoid it.

First, special tax credits can be provided for business firms whose wage bill rises significantly because the minimum wage is increased. That fiscal device is widely used to encourage investment, to promote exploration for oil and gas, and generally to promote business enterprise. Here it would be used to ease the cost pressures on firms heavily affected by an increased minimum wage.

There is a second problem. The program envisaged here will enable the poor to earn a living wage, but middle-and upper-income groups will pay more for the products and services of the present low-wage industries. We envisage a significant shift of real income to the poor from others. At least partial compensation can be achieved by reduced personal income tax rates for low-and middle-income families. These are the groups that would be most heavily affected by higher minimum wages; the upper-middle- (above $15,000 annual family income) and higher-income brackets could well absorb the higher costs. These changes in federal income tax rates would also have the effect of making the tax system as a whole somewhat more progressive.

These measures spell inflation. A large program for public service employment and for manpower training, coupled with tax reductions and tax credits, will themselves help increase aggregate demand and enable the economy to move toward full employment. They would, of course, be supported by the usual instruments of Keynesian fiscal and monetary policy. Reduced spending in other parts of the federal budget may be necessary in order to reduce inflationary pressures, and the chief candidate that suggests itself is military and military-related spending. The policy tradeoff is between world power and economic justice at home.

Economic Opportunity

Unless attention is paid to the barriers that keep racial minority groups in urban ghettos, the program outlined here will have a limited impact. To some extent those barriers can be weakened by geographical dispersion through integrated housing patterns in the suburbs. However, greater progress can be made by eliminating discrimination in employment, for it is there that the most important barriers to equality of opportunity are found. Far more than is now being done can be accomplished by extension of equal opportunity, affirmative action, and related employment programs, especially if they are coordinated with training and education and with public service employment.

For example, many local governments, government contractors, and public agencies have affirmative-action hiring programs in which specific jobs are designated as ones for which blacks or Latins will be hired. Some of these efforts to develop racial balance in employment have been relatively successful, especially when strong administrative pressures have been applied. The basic concept is that blacks and other minorities are hired at all skill levels in approximately the same proportion that they bear to the total labor force in the locality. This approach could well be extended by law to all private employers, not just government contractors. Private business firms could be required to develop affirmative-action hiring programs satisfactory to a human relations office in the local governmental unit, operating within federal guidelines and properly staffed for supervision and enforcement. In this way the opportunity system could move beyond equal opportunity toward positive action that actively seeks out blacks and other minorities. The program has already been successfully tested on a limited scale. The time has come to apply it to the entire private and public sector.

Even this sort of action is bound to raise objections from members of the white majority on the ground that it is essentially a thinly disguised quota system—which it is. The rationale for a general affirmative-action hiring program is that up to now an undisguised and open quota system has been operating in which the black quota in many occupations was zero or close to zero. The result was the phenomenon of crowding discussed in Chapter 5.

This proposal merely would raise the quota to a proportion approximating the nonwhite proportion of the labor force at all levels of employment and in all types of jobs. When combined with programs for full employment and manpower training, it could greatly diminish crowding and widen minority employment opportunities very substantially.[3]

Widened opportunities for minorities is not sufficient by itself, however. Chapter 5 pointed out that blacks and other minorities can move into occupations formerly held by the white majority without significantly altering the crowding of large numbers of the minority into low-wage occupations. If that should occur, the problem will remain, while economic distinctions within the minority come to approximate those of the large society. It is for this reason that affirmative-action hiring programs are at best a corollary to the more fundamental policy of achieving full employment at a living wage for all.

Economic Development

The final element in a comprehensive program to change the economic foundations of the ghetto economy is a program for economic development. Community economic development can itself raise living standards and improve incomes. It can also provide another source of upward mobility for people within the ghetto, But the larger purpose is to shift the outward flow of income, resources, and people that now drain the ghetto of its development potential.

---

[3]A proposal along these lines was made by John Kenneth Galbraith, Edwin Kuh, and Lecter C. Thurow, "The Galbraith Plan to Promote the Minorities," *New York Times Magazine*, Aug. 22, 1971, pp. 9 and 35 ff.

Again, the idea is not new, but the scale on which it is developed would have to be far greater than in the past.

What is needed for an effective community economic development strategy for the inner city ghettos? The first essential is an organized group, widely representative of the inner city, to define acceptable goals and objectives. Control will have to rest with the inner city itself, for otherwise the objectives will be shifted to benefit outsiders.

Second, substantial amounts of capital and other resources will have to be mobilized. Several sources are available, One, with severe limitations, is the earnings, capital, and human resources of the central city. They are difficult to mobilize, but the Black Muslim program shows that substantial progress can come from that source.[4] A second source of capital is the income and capital that now flows out of the ghetto. For example, proposals have been made to expropriate the property of slum landlords who persistently refuse to maintain their buildings. Another possibility is to establish community-owned enterprises to run a legalized numbers game, much as New York State has done with off-track betting.[5] A third source of capital might be grants or interest-free loans—even "reparations" from the outside, via church groups, as demanded by the Black Manifesto developed by James Forman and others and first presented at the 1967 Black Economic Development Conference.[6] Finally, the federal government is a source of capital through federal lending agencies and appropriations under the authority of several pieces of regional economic development legislation. Federal funds have not been available in more than token amounts in the past, however, which is why attention has been given to the other sources mentioned here. There are limits to the resources that can be obrained from local efforts, and meaningful community economic development would certainly require a large federal revenue-sharing program.

---

[4]Little information is available on the extent of economic development fostered by the Black Muslim movement. Casual observation in many inner city areas suggests that some success has been achieved. On the Black Muslim program for economic development, see Elijah Muhammed, *Message to the Blackman in America* (Chicago: Muhammed Mosque of Islam No. 2, 1965), especially pp. 169-186 and 192-201 and E. U. Essien-Udom, *Black Nationalism* (New York: Dell, 1964).

[5]This proposal was made by Daniel B. Mitchell, "Black Economic Development and Income Drain: The Case of the Numbers," *Review of Black Political Economy*, Vol. 1, No. 2 (Autumn 1970), pp. 47-56.

[6]The Black Manifesto, together with James Forman's introduction, is reprinted in *Review of Black Political Economy*, Vol. 1, No. 1 pp. 36-44.

The Politics of Economic Change

One advantage of the economic solutions to the urban racial problem presented here is that they can be accomplished without significant change in individual attitudes toward persons of other races. Whites could continue to hate blacks, and blacks could continue to hate whites. They might have to work together or live near each other because of changed economic relationships, but there need not be any prior change in individual racial attitudes for the program suggested to succeed.

None of these programs or policies are new, and, taken independently, none are revolutionary in either conception or impact. All have been tried before, and most are part of current programs and policies to a greater or lesser extent. But their combined impact would shortly eliminate the inner city ghettos. The inner city would no longer be the home of poverty; the low-wage industries would either have disappeared or would have been transformed into high-wage industries; the low-wage work force will be working for high wages in either public or private employment; economic opportunities will have been widened both through the economy as a whole and within the inner city itself.

Yet when the program proposed here is viewed as a whole, there is no cause for optimism. It would be almost impossible to implement. It envisages such large changes in the economic status quo that it could hardly be expected to obtain majority support at the present time. The political economy of the ghetto is one of a minority held in a dependent position by a majority that benefits economically from the minority's position. As long as the majority is satisfied with the status quo, no major changes can be expected.

One is tempted to draw historical analogies. A traumatic social upheaval on the scale of the Civil War was required to break up the system of coerced labor embodied in slavery. The next pattern of coerced labor, sharecropping and debt tenure, was eliminated under the combined impact of three great social forces, the depression of the 1930s, the economic changes stimulated by World War II, and the technological transformation of southern agriculture. What will it take to eliminate the current pattern of coerced labor embodied in the ghetto economy? Will the majority of Americans willingly give up their favored economic position relative to the racial minorities of the urban ghetto? Probably not, unless they are forced to do so by a social upheaval that reorders basic economic relationships. In this sense, the urban ghettos represent a revolutionary core within

American society whose antagonism will create a continuing turmoil within the larger economic order.

We conclude that there are no practical solutions to the urban racial problem of our time. Workable solutions may be available, and this chapter sketched one that is feasible. There may be others. But if the solutions get to the heart of the problem, if they challenge the existing pattern of economic relations that preserve the inner city ghettos, they have the fatal flaw of political impracticality. The necessary changes will come only when, for other reasons, a crisis occurs in the American political economy that breaks the existing pattern of economic relationships and makes possible some large changes in the patterns that have created our inner city ghettos.

Suggestions for Further Reading

Four paperbacks supplement the economic analyses contained in this book in a variety of useful ways. A large amount of data and other descriptive material is contained in Carolyn Shaw Bell, *The Economics of the Ghetto* (New York: Pegasus Books, 1970), along with a very useful bibliography. Goals, objectives, and policy alternatives regarding the urban racial problem are gathered together in William L. Henderson and Larry C. Ledebur, *Economic Disparity: Problems and Strategies for Black America* (New York: Free Press, 1970). Treatment of the ghetto as a colony is developed in William K. Tabb, *The Political Economy of the Black Ghetto* (New York: Norton, 1970). Finally, Harold G. Vatter and Thomas Palm (eds.),*The Economics of Black America* (New York: Harcourt Brace Jovanovich, 1972), contains a wide variety of readings pertinent to the topics covered in this book.

Two periodicals are useful for following current developments in scholarship on the inner city. *The Review of Black Political Economy*, published by the Black Economic Research Center in New York, is the only scholarly journal strongly concerned with the inner city economy. Most other published material related to that topic is abstracted in *Poverty and Human Resources*, which is the central reference for the highly scattered material available in other scholarly journals. In addition, the *New York Times* is the best source of information on current events as they relate to minority groups and central city problems, but with heavy emphasis on New York City and its metropolitan area.

Those who wish to delve into the ways in which orthodox economists analyze problems of discrimination and their effects should read the two standard treatises on the subject—Gary S. Becker, *The Economics of Discrimination* (Chicago: University of Chicago Press, 1957), and Lester C. Thurow, *Poverty and Discrimination* (Washington: Brookings Institution, 1969). The neoclassical approach pioneered by Becker is developed further in two Rand Corporation reports: Kenneth J. Arrow, "Some Models of Racial Discrimination in the Labor Market" (Santa Monica, Cal.: Rand Corporation, 1971) and Thomas C. Schelling, "Models of Segregation" (Santa Monica, Cal.: Rand Corporation, 1969). One of the best critiques of the neoclassical approach is the review of Becker's book by M. W. Reder in the *American Economic Review*, Vol. XLVII, No. 3, (June 1958), pp. 495-500.